# Other Edens

The Sketchbook of an

# Other Edens

*Artist Naturalist*

## John Henry Dick
*Foreword by S. Dillon Ripley*

The Devin-Adair Company
Old Greenwich, Connecticut

The end papers are a rearrangement of an early print by
SAMUEL HOWITT
(1756-1822)

Copyright ©1979 by John Henry Dick

Library of Congress Catalog Card Number: 79-67270
ISBN: 0-8159-6412-9

Manufactured in the United States of America

# Contents

*To Billy Coleman*
*(1920-1979)*

# Foreword

FEW PEOPLE TODAY, in a relatively short space of years, have seen so much of the wilder parts of the world as John Henry Dick. This sentiment on my part is conditioned by the fact that the author of this volume has *seen* what he has seen.

Ever so many people have trodden in his footsteps, have climbed the tumbled rocks of kopjes or scrambled down cliffs in the Galápagos or searched the marshes of central India, with unseeing eyes, unconscious of the life all around. Most travelers, now so commonly packaged together in tour groups, do not see. They take pictures, of course, and they have "been" there, wherever it is, but their eyes see not nor do their ears hear. Only their mouths speak, and especially later, in the clangor of prideful recitation.

This is not to cast aspersion on anyone. It is only to emphasize the luck of John Henry, born with a desire to look at birds, perhaps the best instinct for the naturalist, or for any observer for that matter — artist, diplomat, confidence man, or certainly sailor or aviator. The skills of observation of everything, from cloud cover to the expressions of people's faces, that come with years of training for looking for birds should never be underestimated. The difference becomes evident when one reads this book and notes how many things the author has seen and retained, sketched in the memory, if not on paper, in his quest for knowledge of birds.

John Henry Dick is one of America's great bird artists. He is also a gentle and a humble, self-reliant traveler in the far places that are left in our shriveling, and increasingly homogenized, planet. These reminiscences tell us much of his passionate quest for peace in nature.

— S. DILLON RIPLEY

*Smithsonian Institution*

# Preface

WHEN I WAS SEVEN I went into the autumn woods near Islip, Long Island, with an air rifle and shot a Golden-crowned Kinglet. Hunting for sport was as much a part of my background as the tall house on 84th Street in New York City, the succession of nannies with odd accents, the variety of tutors. I don't remember having any feeling about killing that tiny bird, only the sense of enormous pleasure I found in its jewel-like beauty. Some time later I experienced the same profound delight in coming upon a male Wood Duck hanging by the kitchen door of my grandparents' house. I relived the same awe I'd felt in looking at the kinglet. The subtle rainbow colors and the exquisite feather patterns moved me more than anything I'd ever known.

In a world where so many people seem caught up in a frantic search for identity and meaning I've come to feel enormously blessed. Perhaps under other circumstances I might have found satisfaction in selling bonds, practicing law or medicine. But, fortunate enough to have a degree of economic security, I was able to pursue my first love — the study and painting of birds.

The happiest part of my childhood, otherwise darkened by family conflicts, poor performance at school, and a painful shyness, was centered on the remaining bits of marsh and woodland around the summer home at Islip. Here I felt an unprecedented freedom. Here I found a wild world of order and beauty that captivated and confirmed me.

It was here, too, that I knew the closest moments with my father. In this setting I ceased to be the disappointing son and he the autocrat. We were companions prowling the 4,000 acres of the Southside Sportsmen's Club, with its pine and oak woods, ponds and clear streams stocked with trout. We shared the thrill and suspense of waiting in a blind, watching Black Ducks circle overhead in late afternoon against the tracery of dark winter branches.

By early adolescence the paraphernalia in my pockets included Chester A. Reed's *Bird Guide*, with its simple, yet vividly rendered paintings of American birds. At thirteen I was allowed, even encouraged, to keep birds in an area of my father's farm. Caring for and raising game birds — quail, pheasant, ducks, and geese — was an invaluable learning experience. It brightened the summer days.

The winters, too, were brightened by constant visits to the American Museum of Natural History. Despite my shyness, I was able to meet outstanding naturalists, men like Frank M. Chapman, James Chapin, Robert Cushman Murphy, and Roy Chapman Andrews. I stood for hours watching Francis Lee Jaques paint his masterful backdrops for wildlife groups in the Oceanic and African halls.

Prep school, from 1932 to 1936, was something of a nightmare. Through no fault of my own I was absent frequently. My grades were disastrous. But due to the perception and kindness of headmaster Frank D. Ashburn I left Brooks School with head held high. He had me paint a mural of local seasonal birds for the wall of the dining hall. It hung there for thirty years; today it hangs in the Art Department.

It was about this time that I discovered for myself the dramatic ornithological compositions of John J. Audubon, the primitive charms of Alexander Wilson, the colorful excitement of John Gould, the observing eye of Louis Agassiz Fuertes. Somewhat later, in Stockholm, I was introduced to the canvasses of that powerful genius, Bruno Liljefors.

During the winter of 1937-38 I visited my mother at a recently acquired winter home in South Carolina. Twenty miles south of Charleston, Dixie Plantation, with its house at the end of a double avenue of moss-hung oaks, faced a wide expanse of marsh and inland creeks, with the Inland Waterway in the distance.

About this time my father, in a stroke of good fortune, employed an unusual tutor for me. John Moffett was truly a man for all seasons, as much at home in the humanities as he was in science. He opened my mind to the treasures of music and great literature. He stimulated and encouraged my study of wildlife. His influence probably prompted me to spend the following two years at the Yale Art School.

The house in South Carolina, completely restored by my mother, burned to the ground in 1939. My mother never returned to it; she died five months later.

The years 1941-45 were a time of compulsory tedium. I was in the Army Air Force, stationed at numerous southern U.S. bases, and finally went to Oahu, then Guam and Saipan. When the war ended I was on Iwo Jima. The fighting over, I was free to explore the island's devastated landscape and the labyrinths of Japanese tunnels. Many "inhabitants," fully uniformed and now badly decomposed, lay about, some still sitting with backs against the walk like discarded mannequins. Although the birding was limited, I remember seeing a few migrants: Red-bellied Rock Thrushes on lava outcroppings, Oriental White-eyes in sheltered, leafy gulleys, and hordes of transient Golden Plover.

After my separation from the military service I left Islip. I had inherited Dixie Plantation, and in 1947 I built my own house there, on a slight rise, looking out on miles of tidal salt marsh. I began painting in earnest, made new friends, and soon was building up a collection of captive waterfowl, pheasants, peafowl, and cranes.

E. Milby Burton, for many years director of the Charleston Museum, introduced me to the finest pockets of wilderness in the Low Country. He also gave me free access to the museum's fine collection of bird skins.

I came to know a particularly rewarding friendship with Alex and Margaret Sprunt. We spent long hours afield together and traveled to the back country of Florida, to the Southwest, and to Mexico. Another friend, Devin Garrity, a New York publisher and nature enthusiast, induced me to illustrate several natural history books.

In 1956 my lifelong involvement with nature took a climactic turn, a first safari in East Africa, where I made my own deeply personal discovery of the wilderness. The years that followed were full of change, involving the transformation of a hunter into a conservationist, and replacing the gun with a camera. But the deepest changes are too profound to describe. The travel sketches that follow can only suggest them.

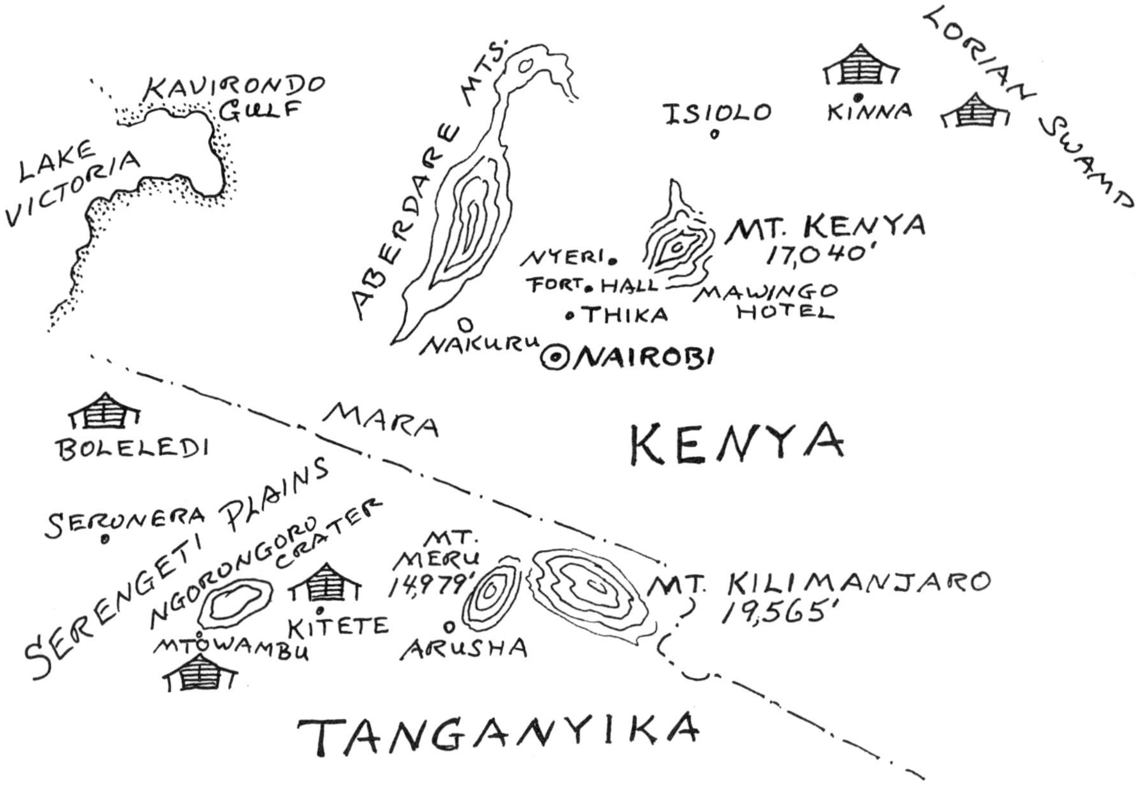

KAVIRONDO GULF
LAKE VICTORIA
ABERDARE MTS.
ISIOLO
KINNA
LORIAN SWAMP
MT. KENYA 17,040'
NYERI
FORT HALL
THIKA
MAWINGO HOTEL
NAKURU
NAIROBI
MARA
KENYA
BOLELEDI
SERONERA
SERENGETI PLAINS
NGORONGORO CRATER
MT. MERU 14,979'
MT. KILIMANJARO 19,565'
KITETE
MTOWAMBU
ARUSHA
TANGANYIKA

# East Africa - Discovery

THOSE WHO SAW wild Africa decades ago tend to say, "Of course, it's all gone now. You should have seen it when I did." This put-down may be partly true, but for the traveler about to visit Africa for the first time enough of the world's greatest wildlife spectacles still remain. Largely unchanged is the wealth of birdlife, the annual Serengeti animal migration, pink drifts of a million flamingos on Lake Nakuru, and the timeless thrill of seeing the golden forms of resting lions, "poured like honey" on the grasslands of the Mara.

I was first drawn to Africa by a fellow Yankee, who, like me, had left the North to settle in Charleston. In 1955 Henry Philip Staats returned from a safari with Sydney Downey, a founding partner of the safari firm of Ker and Downey. Spurred on by Phil's enthusiasm, I signed up with Syd Downey the following year. This was the first of seven safaris. Syd was always the predominant influence, and it was partly through him that my eyes were opened to the beauty and excitement of Africa.

It would be impossible to describe the sights, emotions, and moods of that first safari without touching on the actual hunts themselves. I offer no apology for them. These hunts were restrained and no bloodbath. Game was abundant, and hunting was an accepted part of a visit to Africa. But after the first two safaris I did a complete about-face — the camera replaced the gun, and I found photography equally as exciting.

Since the 1950s time and men have been cruel to the magnificent fauna of East Africa. Recent reports estimate a 90 percent loss of game since the 1940s. In Kenya official hunting safaris were discontinued in 1977, marking the end of an era. Most hunting safaris were mannerly, controlled, and brought helpful revenue to East Africa. They served also to keep a watch on the game, as to both location and numbers. What has resulted, unfortunately, is no better, but worse. The poacher has done far more damage.

A ban on all wild animal trophy sales went into effect in Kenya one year after hunting was discontinued. All curio shops, supposedly cleared of their inventories, were closed. It will be interesting to see what the future is to hold for Kenya's unique wildlife. Except for what remains in the parks, I fear the worst. Even the parks have an uncertain future.

William C. Coleman, a Charleston friend, joined me on that first safari in January, 1956. For years he and I had shared a love of outdoor life as well as a fierce desire to see Africa.

In the pre-jet age the long haul seemed endless — from New York to Rome, Cairo, Khartoum, and Nairobi. Crossing the equator as we

Zebra

... *black crags of Mt. Kenya* ....

approached our destination, the plane passed the black crags and glistening glaciers of 17,050-foot Mt. Kenya, which pierced a thick cloud cover. At the same time, far to the south, just visible 150 miles away, was the great snow cone of Kilimanjaro, Africa's highest mountain, which rises to 19,340 feet.

Syd Downey somehow spotted us as we disembarked from the plane. We shook hands with a lean, darkly tanned man, of medium height and military bearing, who bore a striking resemblance to George VI. Every detail of the drive to town from the airfield remains vivid: the flat plain studded with short, twisted whistling thorn trees, their two-inch spines glistening in the wet like shark's teeth; a few chunky zebra and elegant giraffe loping away from the edges of the dirt road while small Thompson's Gazelles held their ground and, with nervously twitching tails, continued to graze.

Our first view of Nairobi, which is set on a 6,000-foot plateau, was partly obscured by a gray blanket of cold wet clouds. The main streets, many unpaved, were deeply rutted red mud. Groves of eucalyptus rose from hillsides, and flowering trees lined the streets — blue jacarandas, flame of the forest, yellow flamboyants, the pride

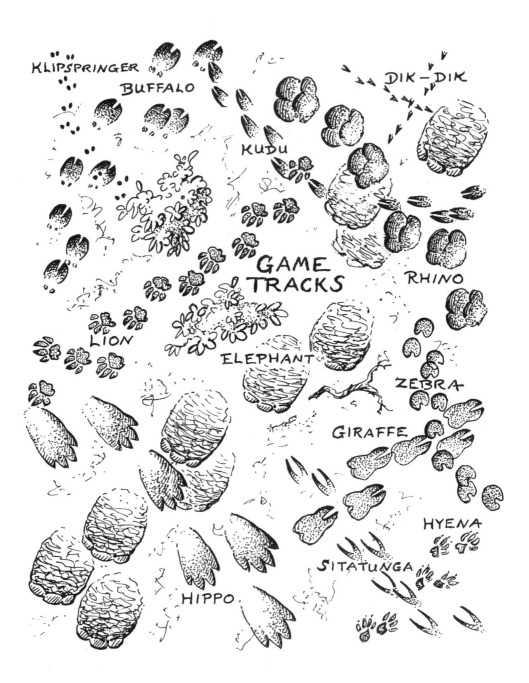

KLIPSPRINGER

BUFFALO

DIK-DIK

KUDU

GAME
TRACKS

RHINO

LION

ELEPHANT

ZEBRA

GIRAFFE

HYENA

SITATUNGA

HIPPO

of India — all exploding with color. The avenue dividers and parks were beautifully landscaped with purple, copper, and red bougainvillea and yellow alamander vines, carefully trained along barbed wire fences.

We checked into Nairobi's oldest hotel, the Norfolk, still one of the most appealing hotels in the world, comfortable, informal, with wonderful food. A large central courtyard held three circular aviaries stocked with noisy, colorful local birds.

Syd gave us a tour of the city, and midway during the afternoon he dropped us at Ahamed's, Nairobi's best safari haberdashery. An hour later Coleman and I emerged outfitted and eager for the hunt. Unfortunately, we looked like extras from a 1930 movie about white hunters. We made a proud entrance back at the Norfolk in our new, overstarched, ill-fitting hunting clothes, and stalked into the Lord Delamere bar.

Surrounded by loud-talking ranchers and hunters fresh from the bush, we ordered drinks with attempted nonchalance. We overheard conversations comparing ivory weights of recently killed elephant, the length of rhino horns, and the problems created by lion running amok on a large sheep ranch. A few of these men wore the leopard-banded tari hats later identified with actor Stewart Granger, but all had well-worn, faded bush jackets smudged with Landrover grease, mud, and occasional flecks of dried blood.

Abashed and self-conscious, we slunk away to the outside terrace café, and asked the Indian bartender to bring us two very dry martinis. Using hand signals, I numbered out ten gins to one of vermouth. The bartender gave me a quizzical look, but nodded in agreement. Minutes later a boy appeared with an overflowing pitcher of martinis — exactly twenty shots of gin to two of vermouth. The bartender must have thought us far tougher than our clothes suggested. Two hours later and in raucous condition we were discreetly led to a table in the far corner of the dining room, half hidden by a screen.

The next morning Syd took us to the Coryndon Museum (now the National Museum), perched near a wooded ravine on the outskirts of the city. Twenty-five years before, he said, this whole area of Nairobi had been rugged wilderness and a favorite place to hunt lion. We were introduced to Dr. Louis B. Leakey, who, though polite, was totally preoccupied with fossil specimens that covered his desk. Since much rain had recently plagued the hunting areas, Syd asked for suggestions. Leakey recommended the Northern Frontier District. He thought this drier area would absorb the recent rains faster than the Mara or Serengeti.

During the British-Italian phase of World War II in Africa, Syd, then in the army, was captured by the Italians and imprisoned in Dessie, Ethiopia. Freed by South African troops and the war over, Syd met his old friend Donald Ker, and, sitting on the steps of the Addis Hotel together, they planned the infant firm of Ker and Downey Safaris Ltd. They gathered a few vehicles, several tents, basic equipment, and went into business. It was the beginning of a partnership that spanned most of their lifetime. Their first job, in 1946, was to lead a large film group into the bush for the filming of Hemingway's *The Short Happy Life of Francis Macomber*.

Syd was the finest kind of hunting companion. Strict and well-disciplined, he hunted by the rules. He respected animals and gave them every possible advantage. One worked hard for what was collected, and little was wasted.

I marveled at his knowledge of tracking. When walking the edge of a water hole or salt lick, I learned that a world of information lay at one's feet, waiting to be read. Identifying tracks of different species became routine. The clarity of the edges of the tracks told within minutes when the animal had been there; even a jumble of many tracks superimposed on each other could be read. When I made a bad shot or wounded an animal, Syd could usually tell where the bullet had hit and if it was fatal by observing the color of the blood, its spacing, and even its height on grass and leaves. A wounded animal that got away was considered as collected. If only one was allowed on the license, that was it.

Eventually, for Syd too, the hunting safari was replaced by trips for photography only. The stalk was now done from an automobile, and here too his ingrained knowledge of tracking was indispensable. The proper approach to a Rosy-patched Shrike in a thornbush required the same care and enthusiasm as stalking one of the big five (Lion, Rhino, Buffalo, Hippo, and Elephant).

Syd had a hearing problem. During dinner questions would go unanswered. Yet I have seen him rise suddenly, aware of a sound inaudible to the rest of us, and go out into the night. There, one hand cupping his ear, he would listen enraptured to the roar of a lion miles away.

A fitting tribute to Syd's reputation was paid shortly before his retirement from the field when he was chosen to guide Prince Charles and Princess Anne on their Kenya safari in 1971.

In 1956 Kenya was still a Crown Colony. The Mau-Mau rebellion was subsiding and under control. What had begun as a black revolution against white settlers backfired. Though fifty or sixty whites were killed, and many more tortured and mutilated, blacks turned on blacks and the insurrection became a tribal war. Hundreds, if not thousands, of Africans died between 1952 and 1956. During the emergency white homes were barricaded at night and black servants locked up in compounds in the evening for their own safety.

During dinner at the Downeys a loaded shotgun was within easy reach, and after the meal all servants returned to the protection of their fenced compound behind the main house.

The trek started from the Norfolk Hotel after breakfast, with Syd's International hunting car in the lead and the packed Bedford truck following behind us.

Hassan, Syd's top camp boy, always traveled with us in the hunting car. A truly remarkable character, Hassan was an ageless Masai—tall, elegant, with a weathered face, one snag tooth, and oriental eyes. As a young man he had been employed at "Karen" by Isak Dinesen. When she returned to Denmark for emotional and financial reasons, Hassan started working for safaris before the modern use of the word was known. In addition to his own tongue, he spoke Swahili, English, and French. When serving dinner at camp he wore a long, white tunic topped by a short, green jacket with gold piping. Traveling with us he dressed in his finest, an ancient army jacket with numerous faded ribbons sewn over his breast pocket. Dinesen, who had trained him from childhood, wrote of their correspondence between Denmark and "Karen." "It was he [Hassan] who was melancholy," and she heard in his letters "the sound of a lonely horn in the woods, a long way off."

As we drove north through the Kikuyu Hills, where numerous villages cling to badly eroded hillsides, sunshine and showers alternated. Smoke spiraled upward from mud-hut villages and small farmhouses with thatched roofs. I was startled by the brilliant blues of Lilac-hearted Rollers perched on fence and telephone wires, almost everywhere. Feathery clumps of giant bamboo were scattered about, and wide-leafed banana trees shone in the wet. Shaven-headed Kikuyu women walked the edge of the road struggling under great bundles of firewood and wattle bark secured to their backs by a head sling. Unburdened men walked or sat by the road gossiping and smoking.

We passed Thika, Fort Hall, Nyeri, and the white highlands with their farms and rolling hillsides of grain on the western slopes of Mt. Kenya. That first night was spent at the deluxe Mawingo Hotel. Its location, at 7,000 feet, was spectacular, with flower-bordered lawns and a sweeping view of cedar-bamboo forests climbing the slopes of Mount Kenya. Unfortunately, the peak was obscured by mists. The second night we camped alongside an abandoned police station, miles from anywhere, with the unfamiliar howls of hyenas and zebra barking far in the distance.

Spotted Hyena

Doum Palms and Thompson's Gazelles

At midmorning the next day we arrived at Isiolo, the clearing station and the last more or less civilized outpost before one enters the vast Northern Frontier District. On the map this seldom-visited area covers the entire northern half of Kenya, from Isiolo and the Tana River north to the Ethiopian-Somalia border. It is a wonderfully wild world of deserts, thornbush plains, dried riverbeds fringed by Doum palms, camel caravans, and rugged mountain ranges. It is the home of nomadic Somali, Boran, and Turkana tribesmen. Though seemingly arid, it is unbelievably rich in wildlife.

Police checked our papers at the barrier and pointed out our next stop, the Game Commissioner's Office. Hidden behind a euphorbia hedge was a small cement hut where George Adamson, the senior game warden, sat at a desk. He was in his late forties, bearded, shirtless, smoked a pipe, and had a twinkle in his eye. We had decided on only one leopard hunting license because Syd was less than enthusiastic about killing the great cats. After some friendly chitchat with Adamson, Billy and I tossed a coin for the license. I lost.

Adamson invited us to his home for a drink. As we entered the simple cement and stone house, we were welcomed by Joy Adamson, a smallish, Austrian-born lady with curly blond hair, wearing shorts and a halter top. She exuded vitality. Caught sweeping the floor, she put away the broom, retired briefly, and reappeared with a tray of glasses, lemon squash, and a bottle of gin. We talked of weather and animals. I remembered she was an artist and asked if we could see some of her paintings.

She led us into the dining alcove, where paintings were everywhere — on the table, hanging, standing against the walls. All were excellent. There were detailed studies of local plants — flowers, leaves, seeds, and root systems — reminiscent of the classic European botanical drawings of the eighteenth century. A small watercolor study of a green chameleon was particularly striking, as were numerous large temperas of native men and women wearing tribal headdresses, body ornaments, and facial markings. I was overwhelmed by her talent. Since tribal regalia is rapidly being replaced by store clothing, these costume portraits should prove invaluable for the future. Many of her plant and tribal studies are now on permanent exhibition at the National Museum in Nairobi.

We walked about outside for a better look at the countryside. The site afforded a view of dry, thornbush country, with its granite outcroppings, distant escarpments, and serpentine riverbeds bordered by green acacia and palms. Far off a circular vortex of vultures rode the heat thermals. Today, largely through the efforts of the Adamsons, this has become the heart of the Samburu-Isiolo Game Reserve.

At one side of the house was a sad, struggling vegetable garden with a few bedraggled flower plants. In her Viennese accent Joy told us, "Gardening here is impossible. When vegetables grow, vat happens? Elephants! Never trouble with bugs, birds, or mice, but always elephants." The house had unfortunately been built astride an ancient, established elephant walk.

I remained outside for a while trying to identify a distant hawk. Walking to the kitchen door, I found myself held at bay by an obese, snarling, yellow-toothed Rock Hyrax, which was sunning itself on the doorsill. This was Joy's devoted pet "Pati." About the size of a football, it appeared to me a decidedly unpleasant little beast.

We left the interesting Adamsons and headed eastward. Exactly one week later George Adamson returned home with the skin of a lioness he had shot in self-defense. With him were three tiny orphaned cubs. One of these was to become the famous Elsa of *Born Free*. I firmly believe that Joy Adamson's book and Rachel Carson's *Silent Spring* have done more to make today's world aware of our relationship with animals and our whole environment than any other literary efforts of this century.

*a typical camp site*

Our first permanent campsite was about a hundred miles southeast of Isiolo, on the plain northeast of Mt. Kenya, in today's Meru Park. This was one of Syd's favorite hunting areas. To me it was the epitome of wild Africa, seemingly untouched, vibrant with creature sounds, and altogether beautiful. Our green tents were shaded by lace-leafed acacia trees and overlooked a meandering, marshy stream called the Kinna. Scattered about and bordering the river were clumps of Doum palms and large, graceful Borassus palms, whose sweet, red fruit was much sought after by elephants. Bold starlings of several species were attracted to camp by bits of bread. They whistled, chattered, and shone in the sunshine like newly cut metal.

But an overpowering mood of death cast a pall over this paradise. Rinderpest, a disease introduced by domestic cattle, had attacked the large Cape Buffalo herds, and the dead and dying were everywhere. In thick bush and tall grass their presence was made known by overhead flights of Cattle Egrets. Carcasses were found by the river's edge, and infected animals stood in deep shade, gaunt, bleary-eyed, saliva streaming from their muzzles. In this condition they can be especially dangerous.

Cape Buffalo

Our camp boys spread the word that we needed a scout. Very shortly there appeared a small brown hunter from the Boran tribe. He had short frizzled hair, and his pierced earlobes stretched down to his shoulders. He wore only a greasy brown blanket, draped over one shoulder Roman style, and carried a spear. Like most primitive people, he was tough, extremely resourceful, and had learned to survive through his knowledge of bushcraft.

We became close companions for several days. When traveling in the car he squatted just behind me, crouched as though ready to spring. His searching, weathered eyes worked every patch of bush for game. His aroma, a combination of rancid animal fat and wood smoke, was more overpowering than unpleasant.

On that first hunt we came across game unique to this part of Africa. Gerenuk Antelope with elongated necks and hides that shone like polished wood broke from hiding and on delicate legs vanished into the bush. We found the Reticulated Giraffe, the most strikingly marked of the five African subspecies; the large-eared, finely striped Grevy's Zebra; Beisa Oryx; and the Somali (blue-necked) Ostrich. On the open plain in the wavering heat of midmorning small herds of antelope grazed.

Having been instructed on the proper technique for stalking, I left the car and walked as low as possible to the ground, rifle in hand. Making my way toward a group of Grant Gazelles, I spotted a passably good head and inched forward from termite mound to termite mound. With mouth dry and heart pounding, I narrowed the distance, then rested my rifle on the crown of a cement-hard mound. Prior to squeezing the trigger my mind suddenly became impersonal — the antelope was not a living animal but simply a target. Through the rifle scope the sharp, black cross hairs met at the shoulder of the Grant. I heard the rifle crack, immediately followed by a plunk sound as the antelope fell. This was the first mammal I had ever killed.

Since we needed meat at camp, the Grant was butchered on the spot. Shortly after this, I collected oryx, waterbuck, and zebra. And though I became hardened to the sight of skinning, butchering, and blood, I never quite learned to accept it.

Having lost the toss for the leopard license, I became an onlooker while Billy went after his prize. Syd remembered a good spot to hang leopard bait. Going on foot through a grassy valley, we came across a massive outcropping of smooth granite boulders called a kopje. Climbing to the top, we looked down on a solitary twisted acacia tree near the base of the sunbaked rocks. We shot a zebra, gutted it, and dragged it as a scent lure, making great circles in the general area. The bait was then pulled to the acacia tree and hoisted by a rope to dangle from a low branch.

*Kopje ... a massive outcropping of stone*

For two consecutive sunrises Billy, Syd, and gun bearer walked a circuitous route to the kopje hoping to find a feeding leopard.

Alone by the hunting car, I found myself for the first time engulfed in Africa. I had never before experienced total wilderness; it produced a feeling of elation mingled with fear. The elation rose from a deep response to the beauty of this trackless land, with its new sights, sounds, and smells. The fear rose from tension at facing the unknown. Even so, I had a sense of homecoming, a profound feeling of belonging, of having been here before. The sun broke out over the distant mountains, pouring golden light on the grass and drying the dew. Somewhere in a nearby valley a White-browed Coucal, the water-bottle bird, gave its strange water-gurgling calls. A trio of giraffe, wearing their knobby horns like coronets, looked down on me from the flat top of a thorn tree. Disturbed by the returning hunters, a cranky Black Rhinoceros, large as a tank and with dried dung caked to his flanks, trotted in front of the car. He stopped, tested the wind, then vanished into the bush.

On the third morning I heard the report of two shots in the direction of the leopard rock. Billy had been presented with a perfect shot. I walked to the scene and found the leopard dead. It had been dispatched neatly as it fed on the maggot-ridden bait. The cat was quickly disemboweled, stuffed with grass, and carried to the car. We all climbed in with it. Now the combined odors of leopard and Boran scout became truly overwhelming. Through clouds of billowing dust, in the midmorning heat, we dodged termite mounds, rocks, fallen logs, and dipped across dry gullies as we raced the ten miles back to camp to skin the leopard before its hair began to slip.

Progress or fate decided that this leopard rock, in the most remote of all places, should become a center of activity for the new Meru Park. On a photographic safari fifteen years later Syd and I found ourselves here again. Several graded roads converged at the granite kopje. The acacia tree where the zebra bait hung was still there. But now a park motor pool spread about the base of the rock. Two red gas pumps, stacked oil drums, and lorries parked in a row crowded it. A small radio tower crowned the rock, while sprawled below in the shade of trees were numerous tents and a new Park Lodge.

The dry bush country of this part of Kenya has always been especially rich in birdlife. Some 332 species have been recorded in the deserts, bush, forests, and swamps of Meru. I will always remember the first bird sound of early morning — the wooden brrrt-brrrt-brrrt of Flappet Larks, African cousins of the skylark, as they rose from the dew-soaked grass, clapping their wings together above their backs to cause this strange unbirdlike sound. The many species of dry bush kingfishers flashed brilliant blue wings in flight. There were noisy hornbills, colorful bee-eaters, rollers, and numerous species of

*morning flight of sandgrouse*

shrikes. Shy, unapproachable Golden-breasted Starlings, the most striking members of their very colorful African family, slipped from tree to tree in loose flocks, trailing magpielike iridescent tails.

Game birds abounded, but hunting them was frustrating and at times ludicrous. The sportiest of all were the plump sandgrouse, coming in the morning to the scarce water holes in the dry riverbeds. In tight compact flocks their clucking calls could be heard from a great distance. Francolin and guineas, both large, chickenlike birds, loathed to fly but could outrun a racehorse. With luck we could corner them in thick grass or surprise them in a small donga ravine. Cold guinea fowl with English mustard made a welcome change from the usual luncheon of tinned corned beef or tongue.

One of the pitfalls of hunting here is the fact that every form of vegetation is equipped to tear, hook, impale, or attach itself. Several kinds of grass seeds, like needles, could work their way through any clothing, and had a special fondness for woolen socks.

An oryx had been shot. After the head skin and neck skin were removed, we dragged the carcass out to an open plain, moved the car into the shade of a tree, and waited. Within minutes circling pinpoints began to collect in the sky, then drop gradually. From miles away others joined the descending dots, and soon great, half-closed wings plummeted to earth with a sound like tearing canvas. The carcass was immediately covered with hissing, flapping, hopping vultures of four species. They resembled ancient hunchbacked crones haggling over a cluster of dirty rags. The smaller Egyptian Vultures, dirty-white, with small chrome yellow heads, were less aggressive than the others and sidled about the perimeter waiting for an opening to join the feast. A Tawny Eagle joined the fray, and Black Kites swooped back and forth stealing morsels from the vultures' bills. Foxlike, silver-backed jackals tiptoed about, stealthily grabbed a scrap of skin or a morsel of meat, then timidly retreated. Had lion or hyena been near, they would have rushed the carcass and forced the birds to roost elsewhere until they had satisfied their appetite.

Helmeted Guinea Fowl

It was my first exposure to this dramatic African spectacle. I marveled at the efficiency of the phenomenon. Only a few large bones were left, and by night these too would probably be carried away. Small mammals, birds, and insects would remove crumbs and juices, leaving the ground clear and greener after the next rainfall.

Safari hours are geared to take the utmost advantage of daylight. This is true whether hunting or photographing. About 5:30 A.M., or one hour before sunrise, the tent flap would be unzipped and a soft African voice would say "Hodi" ("May I come in"). A lantern and a pot of tea would be placed on the ground beside your bed. By the time you were dressed and eating breakfast patches of color appeared in the east. Flappet Larks broke the quiet, then a few doves called, and the morning chorus of birds would slowly build to a crescendo. Occasionally, a lion leaving a night feast and looking for a place to sleep would announce his presence with a few roars.

Vultures cleaning a carcass.

You would then settle yourself and gear into the hunting car and head out. No two excursions were alike. The unexpected became the expected. Mornings were often cold, but as the day progressed the air turned warm and layers of clothing were shed. The drive back to camp about noon was hot, dusty, and thirsty. A light lunch would be followed by two hours of free time, when, unless overcome with sleep, I would often work out a watercolor sketch of a bird collected that morning.

Wildlife activity all but ceases as the midday heat settles over everything. The landscape shimmers in heat waves, and little is heard above the incessant whine of insects. Between three and four o'clock, after another cup of tea, you return to the car, which then heads for new areas if you are photographing, or you may check on a lion or cheetah kill discovered that morning.

As shadows gradually lengthen, the animal world once more awakens and stirs. Antelope leave the shade and feed in the open. Predators stretch, move about, and contemplate the evening's hunt. Woodlands and bush again awaken to the coo of doves, repetitious calls of hornbills, Wood Hoopoes, and the little syncopated tunes of paired barbets, the two sounding like one.

At sundown you are back again in camp. The shower is crude but effective. Water heated in ten-gallon oil tins is poured into a canvas bag with a shower head attached. This arrangement is hung from a branch and enclosed in a small canvas tent. Bathed, you find freshly laundered clothes laid out on your cot. Dressed and content, you pour yourself a drink, pull up a camp chair by the fire, review the day, and plan for the morrow.

Evening is Africa's finest moment. With only a brief twilight, the setting sun seems to pull a star-speckled, velvet-black blanket over the sky. Cool air moves in. The last coo of the dove is heard. Bush Babies, tiny, large-eared nocturnal primates, wail in the thorn trees, and somewhere near or far owls call.

During our supper, in good weather, the sides of the mess tent were left open, and moths, termites, and large sausage ants (flying termites) swirled about the hissing Coleman lantern suspended from the tent pole. It was part of our routine that after coffee Syd would formally excuse himself, retire to his tent, and write up the daily log. More often than not I would carry my chair from the mess tent back to the fire.

I loved most of all this private moment at the end of an African day. Kicking the unburnt log ends into the center of the glowing coals, I would sit quietly, reveling in the sounds — a strange, wild, natural symphony with its own distinct themes, counterpoint, and harmony. From somewhere behind would drift the soft singsong voices of the Africans talking together as they cleaned the supper dishes and prepared for sleep, gentle, musical sounds without a harsh syllable.

Cricket calls were everywhere; in the distance a zebra might bark. Elephant, with their uncanny powers of scent and their respect for man, never actually walk into camp unless ill or deranged (a rogue), but in the bush country swishing sounds, soft rumbles, and the sharp crack of a branch might indicate their presence. A rare and thrilling night sound would be the harsh cough of a prowling leopard, like the distant rasp of a saw on wood. The eerie woooup-woooup-woooup of hyena was a common sound.

But the dominant sound in the African darkness is the roar of the lion. It has no rival, and what a majestic, arrogant sound it is! As a pride moves over the land, each animal roars at his own tempo as they begin their evening's hunt. The full roars are variable, often muffled and difficult to locate, but the deep, soft, coughing grunts at the end of the roar betray the location of the beast. Many an evening, sitting by the fading coals, I held my ground as just beyond the wall of light lions approached unseen. Common sense would then drive me to the safety of my thin canvas tent. In the morning tracks could be seen in the cooled wood ashes, sometimes as close as a foot from the tent itself.

On our last afternoon at camp on the Kinna River Billy and I were favored with a prime example of British understatement. Just before the afternoon hunt a lorry drove up loaded with armed black militia and a British officer at the wheel. Syd recognized the officer and invited him for tea. No mention was made of his reasons for being in the vicinity. After talk about everyone's favorite subject, game and wildlife, and with the teapot empty, the Huntley and Palmer biscuits consumed, the officer returned to his lorry. Resting one foot on the side of the vehicle, he remarked to Syd, "I forgot to mention, Syd, that we are here on Mau-Mau patrol. Several of the troublesome chaps have been captured already." Then, pointing to a distant burning hillside, he added, "Thought our ring of fire would round them up, but three have escaped. Their logical route from the fire would be along this stream, bringing them by your camp sometime during the night. If you do see them, shoot them for us." Then, with the truck door closed and motor running, he called back, "So long, Syd. Cheerio, and good hunting! Thanks for tea!"

At sunrise all twelve safari boys were busy dismantling the camp, carefully folding canvas and tying up tent poles. Numerous heavy green boxes stenciled "Ker & Downey," packed with foodstuffs, china, silver, glasses, and such paraphernalia, were loaded beside water and oil drums in their proper places on the Bedford truck. Syd, very much the military man, paced the area nervously snapping orders, as a general might before a convoy takes to the field. Once the truck and car were packed, all the gear was covered by tarpaulin secured by ropes, necessary to keep out the major curse of a safari, dust. The safari boys would sit on the tarpaulin and ride hanging onto the ropes for dear life.

We headed for the Lorian Swamp two hundred miles to the northeast. I have been told that here in 1909 Theodore Roosevelt, on a long and grueling foot safari, collected several large elephants. Syd recalled that on another safari long ago he had never seen any marsh harbor so many duck. As the hours passed, the terrain became drier and more desolate. Wild plains animals thinned out, giving way to herdsmen with hordes of goats, fat-tailed sheep, donkeys, and camels. The camels wore large wooden bells that gave a loud, clanking noise.

We noticed several rutted tracks that converged at a jumble of metal-roofed mud huts. The only spots of color in this tan world of dust and sand were brilliant red signs tacked to the adobe walls advising "Drink Pepsi-Cola." Some promoter had arrived long before the distributor, for when we asked if the drink was available, nobody had ever seen a bottle.

Stopping an aloof, fine-featured but sinister-looking Somali, Hassan asked the name of the town and if there were any palm oases ahead where we might camp for the night. Garba Tula was the town, and we were headed on a treeless route.

We continued into the desert, searching for a donga or dried riverbed that might offer some shelter from sudden windstorms.

Random piles of white bones dotted the landscape, reminders of migratory domestic herd animals that had perished during periods of drought.

Late in the afternoon, far to the north, we made out the long green fringe of the Lorian swamp. We brought our two vehicles to a halt. Enough sticks and dried dung were gathered to build a small fire, and we cooked the evening meal and made camp.

An oversized molten sun settled behind the marsh. The air stilled, and the heat became oppressive. We watched long strings of water birds flying over the marsh, black silhouettes against an orange-red sky. A gray fog rose from the swamp and quickly spread in every direction. Soon we found this cloud to be swarms of mosquitoes. The only escape from torture was to crawl under the mosquito bar suspended by upright wires over our cots, stare through the mesh at the vaulted constellations overhead, and sweat the night out. Our safari boys, either because of body chemistry, long association, or self-discipline, never complained about the insects.

With the coming of dawn and the arrival of a breeze the mosquitoes withdrew into the swamp. We walked some distance along the edge of the marsh, expecting myriads of duck to break from wet places, but saw only a few Gargany Teal, White-faced Whistling Ducks, and a handful of Knob-billed Geese. Far in the distance the serpentine trunks and flapping ears of feeding elephant could be seen.

Faced with the fact that a duck hunt was not to be, we left the area and headed back toward Nairobi.

We crossed a flat desolate plain broken by groves of scattered acacia trees. Looking over several male Grant Gazelles, we were suddenly conscious of their exceptionally fine heads. One in particular was a handsome specimen with fantastically tall, gracefully turned horns. Syd said, "My God, that has to be a world's record. We must get it." His well-concealed trophy lust could be contained no longer.

It was my turn to hunt, so, leaving the car, gun in hand, I walked, crouching low, toward the nervous antelope. Three times, from a sitting position with my gun resting on my knee, I lined up the cross hairs of the scope and fired. Three cracks from the rifle resulted in three puffs of dust that prompted the gazelle to move away faster.

*a fine Grant Gazelle*

Syd, walking a few paces behind me, was frantic at the thought of losing such a magnificent trophy. Frustrated, I watched my last chance evaporate, when suddenly the animal stopped, lowered its rear and relieved itself. It was not very sporting, I admit, but I shot at once. Today its handsome head graces my studio wall. The length of the horns is 29 inches, at that time just a quarter-inch short of Roland Ward's list of world's records.

In three days of hard driving we retraced our route through Isiolo, Nanyuki, Nairobi, and went on into Tanganyika (now Tanzania). I recall the bustling activity of Arusha — white farmers and families in town to shop, cold Tuska beer, hot curried Indian samosas (sold at the bar), and tall, elegant Masai striding barefoot down the street. Shaven-headed women wore massed circular copper necklaces, and pounds of metal bracelets tightly entwined their arms. Thin, aloof men sported black ostrich plumes in their hair, bobbing to the rhythm of their graceful gait.

From Arusha the deeply rutted Great Northern Road brought us to a temporary campsite deep in a great forest at the base of the Ngorongoro Crater escarpment. Alongside the road were a few small plantations of taro, corn, and bananas. Wattle huts were scattered among the crops.

Camp was set up in a forest clearing, a new world of towering trees and dank undergrowth, echoing with sounds. There was the heavy woof-woof-woof wingbeats and braying calls of Silver-cheeked Hornbills; the flutelike notes of the White-browed Robin Chat, cooing calls of a Narina Trogon, and the distant squeals of feeding elephant. But the most persistent noise was eerily human; it came from a large troop of rank-smelling baboons who had set up house-keeping nearby at the end of a large dead branch. Their general chattering, grunts, whoops, and screams never abated. Like the closing bars of a Charles Ives symphony, the final cacophony was cataclysmic when a visiting baboon joined the clan and his extra weight proved more than the branch could bear. With a loud crack it broke, and visitor, troop, and branch all crashed to the jungle floor.

We traveled up the escarpment in low gear, inching our way along steep switchback curves. Leaving the hillside farms behind, we entered the cloud forest that bordered the rim of Ngorongoro Crater. Tall trees with suspended lianas and banners of Usnea lichen ap-

... the Ngorongoro Crater ...

*Narina Trogon*

peared ghostlike out of the mist, only to vanish as another cloud moved in.

During bright periods the forest was ablaze with crimson-flowering tulip trees, pink cape chestnuts, and others whose names I didn't know. Small active sunbirds of five species — Scarlet-chested, Bronzy, Golden-winged, Variable, and Double-collared — flashed brilliant metallic colors as they fed on the blossoms. As we walked through thick bracken undergrowth to reach the crater's rim, tall weeds with woolly leaves stuck to our clothing.

We peered down into perhaps the world's largest caldera. Fingers of forest spilled over the rim of the crater, and game trails zigzagged to the valley below. Violet cloud shadows slipped down the 2,000-foot walls and traversed the flat, multicolored floor of grass.

In dry weather the crater supports one major lake, but now, after so much rain, the floor shone like scattered bits of broken mirror. Syd realized it would be impossible to negotiate the only tract to the floor, difficult under the best of conditions. Disappointed, I had to content myself with gaping at the massed game herds through binoculars. Even at a height of 2,000 feet we could identify grazing wildebeests and zebra, locate the tawny shapes of resting lion and the dark chunky forms of rhino.

Next morning we gradually descended over the north rim toward the Serengeti plain. We passed Olduvai Gorge, which the Leakeys were to make famous, and moved on to the Serengeti itself.

At noon the safari came to a halt at an outcropping of granite boulders standing alone in the middle of the open plain. Before climbing its 200-foot height, we circled the base to check for lion or

Secretary Bird

.... *horder of wildebeest.* ....

leopard, who often frequent such vantage places. Finding nothing but a few timid Rock Hyrax, we walked up the rocky slopes and, with a sandwich in hand, sat on a flat stone and marveled at the parade before us.

As far as the eye could see shifting herds of game, six or ten abreast, like veins in green marble, flowed in seeming rivulets, streams, and rivers, moving on to new grass. Grant and Tommy, Topi and Eland were almost always in view. Zebra passed by in gray hordes, but by far the most abundant were the sad-faced, moaning wildebeest. All took part in this incredible journey, crossing the Serengeti en route to the central plains and the corridor near Lake Victoria. Furtive jackals and droopy-rumped hyenas followed the herds, on watch for a newborn calf or its afterbirth, and always waiting for the sick and the dying.

Several times during our trek we spotted a solitary Secretary Bird and the giant Kori Bustard, like camp followers walking with great dignity near to the herds, awaiting insects, reptiles, or rodents disturbed by the animals' feet.

Scattered spirals of vultures smudged the cloudless sky, and directly overhead a large-headed, stub-tailed Bateleur Eagle tilted its wide wings, showing the black primaries and white wing lining. Yellow-throated Sandgrouse by the hundred flushed in front of the car and in leapfrog fashion settled beyond the next upcoming flock.

Nowhere else on earth can one still see so many animals in the wild. I remember a feeling of strange nostalgia, and an even stranger aura of serenity, as if thrust backward in time, privileged to enter a Pleistocene world.

We headed for Seronera, headquarters for the Serengeti National Park. Thirty miles beyond brought us to a lovely area called Boleledi. Syd had a hidden campsite near here of which he was especially fond. We drove off the main track and stopped the car. With branches we swept away all traces of our tracks and erased any evidence of where we had turned off. Most hunters in those days had their private hideaways affording a fine view, plenty of game, and available water. Downey seldom told Ker of his secret places and vice versa.

One could easily see the reason for such secrecy. This spot had a back-country, New England look about it, with gentle hills, forest patches, rocky outcroppings, grassy meadows, and blue-barked angular trees that resembled abandoned apple orchards. In the wonderful week we spent here, hunting and photographing, we never saw another human being.

I always remember this spot as the camp of the lions. During the early days of the safari we had often heard lions, but we had not met up with any. Here, unmolested, lions were common.

Lions fascinate almost everyone. I suppose it is the appeal of looking on the earth's ultimate predator (excluding man). Whether it is its size, dignity, strength, or ruthlessness, the male lion seems the unquestionable symbol of total power, the king of the beasts.

Once, shaving before supper, I heard a large pride pass close by. Their roaring was magnificent. I happened to look into the tin washbasin, and to my utter amazement I saw concentric sound waves breaking the surface of the soapy water. I had been told that under the right conditions the roar of a lion can be heard for ten miles. I believe it.

Syd remembered seeing three superb, black-maned lions that generally lived and hunted in this vicinity. Though now past their prime, they dominated their world from the summit of a hill, complete with rock castle and shady fig tree. By special permission from the government, an important Near East potentate had recently shot one of the three. The loss of this handsome beast shocked and enraged Downey. With years of lion hunting behind him, he has watched their numbers decline. It irked him to remember the many well-heeled, badly trained clients wounding and making a shambles out of an easy hunt. The thought of killing a lion was now totally repugnant to him.

With little trouble we found the two remaining companions at the expected place. Syd decided they needed a meal. A wildebeest, abundant in this area, was shot. A rope was strung through the hocks. The carcass was then dragged two or three times in the wide circle about the lions, and left. Picking up the scent, the lions trotted up to the bait, ripped open the visceral cavity, and began to feed. They fed first on the gonads, then the innards, and discarded the

... *Two remaining companions* ...

stomach with its bushel of spilt fermented grass. We returned to the spot several hours later and found most of the carcass eaten. All that remained was the skin, rib cage, and head. At the sound of our car, two great shaggy, contented lion heads appeared above the windblown grass, muzzles red with blood, eyes glazed with contentment. Anne Lindbergh described looking into the face of a lion: "When they turn their sultry, amber eyes on you, the light is alien and comes from another world."

During a subsequent morning's drive we unwittingly passed between a young male lion and the grazing Thompson's Gazelle he was stalking. Inching his way, close to the ground, muscles taut, he was about to make the final rush when we rumbled by and alerted the gazelle. The disgruntled lion slunk away toward the shade of thick bush, dragging an injured leg. Syd was very upset by our bad timing. Later in the morning Billy shot an Eland bull; he wanted the horns and the camp needed meat. Recalling the limping lion, Syd tossed a haunch into the car, and we went to find him. Remembering an old trick, he secured the meat to a rope attached to the car. Locating the lion, we dropped the haunch to the ground. The lion, rising from his lair, rushed it, grabbed the meat, and tried to pull it away. A tug-of-war ensued, and despite the injured leg, the cat was able to pull our hunting car backward for several feet. We then slipped the rope and drove off leaving him in peace.

According to an ancient Somali proverb, "A brave man is always frightened three times by a lion; when he first sees his track, when he first hears his roar, and when he first confronts him."

This provided little consolation when the three of us confronted twenty-two lions during a leisurely afternoon's trek. Walking about a parklike area, gun in hand, we hoped to collect francolin for the pot.

I noticed not too far away an outcropping of boulders spotted with tawny shapes sprawled in various positions. My binoculars revealed about two dozen lions watching our every move. With palms wet and the hairs at the back of my neck bristling with tension, following Syd, we took a long circuitous route back to the safety of camp.

Our last camp was not far from Lake Manyara, and the village of Mtowambu, Tanganyika, at a place called Kitete. It was a spectacular location, with the Ngorogoro escarpment to the west and the two

*a large Baobab Tree*

great volcanic mountains, Meru and Kilimanjaro, to the northeast. Only at sunrise, with the atmosphere clear of haze, would those two giant lavender cones (Meru superimposed upon the even greater Kilimanjaro) appear.

Sleeping sickness had recently broken out locally, causing the Masai and their cattle to leave the area. Along with the numerous tsetse flies, we had the hills, woodlands, plains, and marshes to ourselves. Some of the largest and most grotesque Baobab trees I have ever seen in Africa were in this area. We drove about, hunted a little, photographed, and bemoaned the fact that the safari was over.

The end of a safari always confronts me with conflicting emotions — happy memories and sad, a special kind of fulfilment overcast with reluctance to leave Africa. This time I was sharply aware that my friend Syd was a worried man. The pressures and frustrations of living in a changing East Africa were taking their toll. He had to deal daily with increasing government restrictions and red tape. He was forced to watch the unrelenting disappearance of the game. The old order had gone forever and, with it, his world. I could offer no reassurance, torn between affection for this extraordinary man and the realization of the weakness of the white man's claim. True, our view, our esthetic appreciation, of the wildlife differed radically from that of the Africans. But was it not, after all, their heritage, their country, their game?

Over the past weeks Syd's conversation had turned again and again to lion, that ultimate symbol of the free wilderness. On one last sortie in this magnificent country we happened on a lone lioness walking with her cub. We watched them for a long time without speaking. I remember, as we turned to go, Syd, looking back, his voice barely audible, "Take care . . . God be with you."

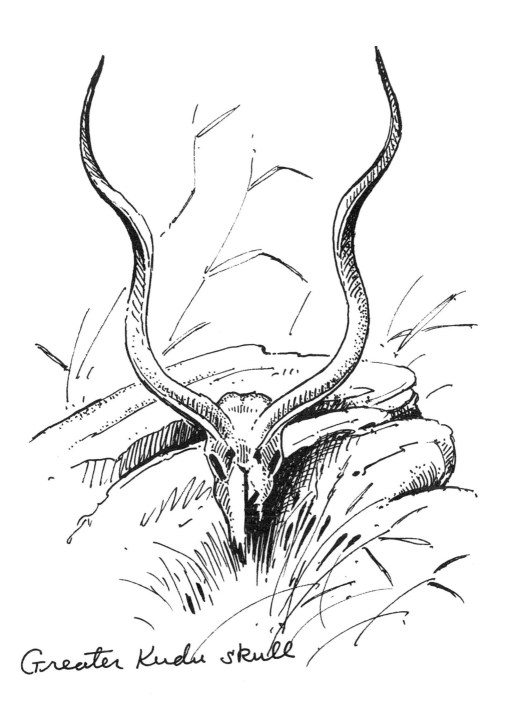

Greater Kudu skull

ETHIOPIA
SUDAN
LAKE RUDOLF
SOMALIA
MARSABIT
UGANDA
CONGO
KENYA
LAKE ALBERT
LAKE GEORGE
MERU
LAKE NAKURU
LAKE VICTORIA
ISHASHA
NAIROBI
RWANDA
MT. KILIMANJARO
MALAGARASI
BURUNDI
UJIJI
ARUSHA
MOMBASA
TABORA
LAKE TANGANYIKA
TANGANYIKA
ZANZIBAR
DAR ES SALAAM

# East Africa II

DURING THE FIFTEEN years between 1956 and 1971 I made eight trips to East Africa. Seven were safaris with Syd Downey as white hunter, guide, and friend. The second safari, to Tanganyika, had its bloody moments. Days of difficult hunting produced a fair Sable, an excellent Greater Kudu, and an elusive Sitatunga. My third safari with John Williams, one of Africa's top naturalists, was devoted entirely to bird collecting and photography. Four more photographic safaris followed. Each in its way was equally challenging.

## Hunting Sitatunga

Billy Coleman and I returned to Tanganyika during the summer of 1959. We had become too competitive on the first safari. Both of us recognized this. Whose impala had the longest horns? Who shot more guinea fowl from a flock? Such things became far too important. Hemingway based his book *The Green Hills of Africa* on this theme. Competition is an important and desirable drive in most sports, but not in hunting and fishing. These, I believe, should remain individual experiences.

On this 1959 safari Syd took on another white hunter, John Kingsley Heath, and doubled the safari staff and equipment, freeing us to pursue different interests.

We all met at the Tabora airstrip in southwestern Tanganyika. The town is located at a crossroads where ancient slave and ivory trading routes met. Arab dealers and buyers with their slave caravans once converged here, and legend has it that the roads approaching Tabora are paved with the bones of their chattels.

From the plane's small window as we descended I recognized Syd holding his familiar wide-brimmed hat with its rumpled black ostrich feather stuck in the band.

Early in the present century, when Tanganyika was a German colony, Tabora had been chosen as the site for a hunting lodge for Kaiser Wilhelm II. This lodge was now a hotel. The white proprietress could have been a character from a story by Somerset Maugham. Caught in a web of boredom, living in this remote community, she asserted herself by dyeing her hair a brassy hue, using heavy stage makeup, and flashing silver nails. She always had a bottle at hand. Her husband, equally trapped, regaled anyone at the bar with endless tales of elephant hunting.

In this setting of faded rustic grandeur, overhead paddle fans, dusty, mounted trophy heads, and colorful characters we discussed and planned our upcoming safari. A few days before our arrival

Kaiser's Lodge at Tabora

Heath had flown over likely hunting areas and decided that the swamps near the Malagarasi River, considerably west of Tabora, were the most favorable for our purpose. Because of the distance and the terrible road conditions, it was decided to transport the whole operation by train. This meant twenty boys and four vehicles would travel on flat cars, and Coleman, Dick, Downey, and Heath would rough it in the caboose.

Syd had often spoken of the elusive Sitatunga, and by now it had assumed almost legendary proportions. We now headed for its habitat. This was also good country for sable and kudu.

Sitatunga are the only truly aquatic African antelope. Handsome, little known, and very shy, a few still inhabit the vast central African swamps. In the past they were abundant on the many islands in Lake Victoria. About the size of our Virginia deer, Sitatunga have thick shaggy coats, tightly spiraled horns, and white harness markings that betray their close relationship to kudu and bushbuck. Living in the impenetrable morasses of floating vegetation, they have evolved very long hooves, which support their weight when they walk on these watery platforms.

With luck they are sometimes seen grazing and browsing in early morning and evening on dry land, but when frightened they vanish into the swamps. If pursued, they will swim with head held well back and nostrils just showing above water.

After a long, uncomfortable, and sleepless night in the caboose, we arrived at the whistle-stop station of Malagarasi. Cars and trucks were driven off the flatcars, and the double safari headed for the wilderness.

It was now the dry season and smoke was everywhere, possibly caused by lightning, but more probably by natives. Miles of woodland had been burned, and here and there a trunk or log still glowed red, white smoke curling upward in the still, hot air. Dust devils, spawned by heat, like whirling dervishes skipped and danced through the dry, leafless Brachystegia woodlands.

Since there were no roads, we made our own. Logs and stones had to be moved and brush cut as we slowly went our way. The silence of the forest was broken by the constant whine of locusts and occasionally the whistle of an oriole or the clear calls of White-headed Black Chats.

*a Nyamezi bee hive*

Billy hoped to shoot a bull elephant, and everyone became conscious of their nearness and numbers in the area. In the early morning coolness fresh dung still gave off steam. Heath and Syd would insert their hands into the large "loaves" to feel the inside temperature, from which they could ascertain the exact time when they had been dropped. Elephants were often seen, but none showed ivory of shootable size.

We came across several hunters from the Nyamezi tribe with their dogs. These lean, lanky men strangely resembled the angular trees and branches and blended perfectly into the forest. Their sole mission, it seemed, was to check the elongated baskets they had hung in the crotches of trees for bees. When an active hive was found, they removed bees, grubs, comb, and honey, and mashed it all into a sticky paste. Some of it they ate on the spot; the remainder they carried home.

Once settled at camp, Syd and I made routine checks of the edge of the local swamps for Sitatunga. We had little success. Only one or two reddish does and fawns were seen. But Heath refused to be thwarted and devised a plan. His idea was simple: drive a car over the railroad bridge. He was sure this could be done if the wheels on one side rode the iron rail and the other two bumped along over the crossties. I was rather amazed that Syd went along with this plan.

Packed with hunting and camping gear, food, gas, and water, the car set forth with the four of us and Mbitu, Syd's number one boy. Scrambling up the crushed rock shoulders of the roadbed, we headed across the 600-foot trestle. Almost immediately things went wrong. The wheels could not be kept on the rails. When we were over the actual river, there was no rock bed between the crossties. The spaces between were far too great to allow the car to move forward. When the safari boys put wooden planks across the ties, the car lurched forward, stopped while the planks were leapfrogged ahead, then continued. It was a slow, laborious process.

Twenty feet below the muddy river swirled. Several times the crossties broke under the weight of the car. The ancient timbers (cut by the Germans sixty years before) might handle the evenly distributed weight of a train, but not ours.

After an hour and a half the car was midway over the span. Someone then remembered that the morning train from Ujiji to Tabora might be due at any moment. The approach to the bridge was around a long curve, so that when the train saw our predicament, there would be little time to stop. Billy and I went a considerable distance ahead on the track. We planned to wave a towel to warn the train when it appeared. Luckily the train was running late that morning and by the time it arrived we were safely off the track and heading for the swamp.

We drove about for two days and failed to see any Sitatunga in the sea of tall marsh grass. Heath thought about future hunts and envisioned green plains teeming with game. So he set fire to streamers of toilet paper, which he released in the 18-foot elephant grass, which is highly combustible. Soon it was crackling and ablaze with towering flames. I thought it a very dangerous procedure. Had the wind shifted I doubt that we could have outrun the wall of fire.

We retraced our tortuous route across the railroad bridge without mishap and returned to the Malagarasi camp.

Checking the swamp edges the next morning, I could hardly believe my eyes when I saw a buck Sitatunga sporting good horns. We hastily devised a plan. Billy and I would stand in the swamp. A good distance apart, near open areas, we would wait and watch. Heath, with his group of safari boys, sloshed into the water at the far side and exploded thunder flashes, powerful firecrackers used to rout elephants from planted crops and cane shambas.

After the first blast a whirlwind of storks, ibis, and herons flapped away in all directions. When the noise ceased, now waist deep in water, I noticed the tall papyrus stalks ahead of me begin to tremble slightly. Then the feathery, tipped reeds parted, and thirty yards away a buck Sitatunga daintily stepped out into the open. He paused

Sitatunga in papyrus

and looked about carefully. My gun was up, and I was ready. I made a good heart shot, and the buck fell on the floating mat of grass. I waded up to the animal. It had a handsome head with lyre-shaped, ivory-tipped horns. Five safari boys lifted the Sitatunga high over the grass and carried it out of the swamp and back to camp.

We broke camp and retraced our way to the railway station, returning to Tabora by the next train.

## Lake Nakuru

Few spectacles are more thrilling than the birdlife on Kenya's unique Lake Nakuru. From a distance this circular shallow lake mirrors white cloud formations on glassy green waters while pale pink drifts of Lesser Flamingos — sometimes as many as two million — are massed along the contours of the lakeshore.

My first view of Lake Nakuru in 1964 could not have been under more favorable circumstances. John Williams had been given free access to trespass on "Nderit," owned by Lord and Lady Hamilton. This property included at that time the entire southern and southeast sides of the lake. With Williams as guide, Syd Downey, the Colemans, and I drove up to the house.

Here was certainly the best of two worlds. The beauty of a small English estate, with a formal rose garden, all in perfect taste. The house was perched high on a hilltop, overlooking one of the world's most beautiful wildlife sights.

Standing on the front lawn and looking skyward, I gazed at lazy spirals of hundreds of White Pelicans riding the thermal drafts high above the lake. Turning in slow motion, the birds changed from blinding white to dark as they circled from full sun to shadow. Below the terrace garden a grassy plain sloped toward the lakeshore. Spotted over the lush grass were small groups of waterbuck, impala, Thompson's Gazelles, and dairy cattle. These seemed out of place among their wild ungulate relatives. Clumps and small woodlands of yellow-barked Fever Trees bordered the white lakeside flats. From a distance these stately trees recalled the champagne glass shapes of our disappearing American elms.

We drove down the hill and walked to the water's edge. Tens of thousands of flamingos took to the air with a gabbling roar, circled about on outstretched wings, then glided off to other feeding sites miles away. Seen in flight, their open, crimson, black-tipped wings showed them to be much redder than when feeding with their wings tucked in.

I gathered my camera gear and walked across the crusty, white, soda shore, crossed over a narrow highwater band of pink flamingo feathers, and waded ankle deep in tepid water to a small grassy islet. Here, like an animal about to make its bed, I stamped on the earth, flattened the grass, and opened up small viewing spaces. I then settled down to wait.

Black-winged Stilts, Ruffs, and stubby Little Grebes returned to the area within minutes. With a swoosh of wings and splashes, a small flock of speckled Cape Wigeon landed ten feet away and resumed their feeding in the soupy water.

It was at least an hour before I was conscious of flamingos returning. Their distant gabbling and honking increased, and soon, as though engulfed by an advancing tidal wave, I was completely surrounded by them. Poking the camera lens through the grass I had no trouble photographing the birds. In some instances they were much too close for my 400-mm lens. I was thrilled by their proximity and the loud contented sounds they made while feeding. Even the strong odor of excrement and churned-up lake muck was not unpleasant. I remained almost motionless for another hour, watching the lovely creatures feed, preen their rosy feathers, and move slowly about undisturbed.

Finally, out of film, wet with sweat, my legs badly cramped, I stood up. Thousands of gracefully curved necks shot up. Innumerable small red eyes looked at me and at each other. Danger was present. I wondered which birds would sound the alarm and panic first. Nothing happened for several seconds; then a small group on the outer fringes flew off. They were followed immediately by a thunderous explosion. The air became a psychedelic jumble of long necks, dangling legs, and flapping crimson wings. The birds then regrouped in loose crisscross formations and disappeared across the lake.

It takes a staggering quantity of food to satisfy more than a million flamingos, along with thousands of pelicans, herons, ibis, ducks, and the rest. Unique Lake Nakuru is shallow. About twelve square miles in size, it has no outlet. Its high concentration of minerals and soda is due to evaporation and the leaching of nearby volcanic soils that drain into its basin. Water is fed into the lake by natural springs and rainfall. Because of the strong mineral concentration no plant life can exist in its waters except for a blue-green algae that thrives under these special conditions.

Flamingos spend most of their time resting and feeding. It has been estimated that here they consume over 150 tons of algae daily. When feeding, their heads are held upside down. A specialized tongue system in the bill works like a rapid piston pump, bringing in algae-laden water, then pushing it out through the superfine combs, like whale baleen. The algae is retained and the water is expelled.

Lesser Flamingos, by far the most abundant of the five known species, only feed on Lake Nakuru; they do not breed there. Nevertheless, I have seen their conical mud nests in scattered groups of up to perhaps thirty. I have even seen an egg or two, but these attempts proved to be abortive.

These birds range the soda lakes of the entire East Africa Rift valley but generally breed only on Lake Natron, south of the Kenya-Tanzania border.

...flamingos ... Lake Nakuru...

The fragile ecology of Lake Nakuru could easily be destroyed by the chemicals and sewage that pour into the lake from the rapidly expanding city of Nakuru. Happily, one chemical plant manufacturing copper oxychloride has recently promised to relocate.

Although the Lake Nakuru National Park (the first park in Africa set aside for its birdlife) has attracted worldwide interest and donations, and though its size has been increased from 14,000 to 50,000 acres, its future remains in constant jeopardy. Only when and if Kenyans realize what a unique and important treasure they have will the future of the park be secure.

At Lake Nakuru there are always endless possibilities for a bird photographer. Large groups of white pelicans, with brilliant yellow bills and shell-pink washed plumage, roost on sandbars. They fish on the water, trapping their prey with the efficiency of a purse net. Like an aquatic ballet, all heads slowly submerge at the same time, then reappear, with their huge bill pouches filled with minnows and talapia.

Hunchbacked Marabou Storks, suggesting illustrated characters from a Dickens novel in their ungainly dignity, walk the shore, hoping to make a meal from a sickly or dying flamingo. Numerous Yellow-billed Storks, African Spoonbills, and Greater Flamingos tower above their smaller, redder relatives. Handsome black-and-white Blacksmith Plovers give loud metallic calls when disturbed from sandbars and flats.

Driving along the western shore under the baboon cliffs and flood-killed trees that hug the edge of the lake, I would find cormorants and African Darters drying their outstretched wings in the sun, herons of several species, and, of course, the glorious African Fish Eagle. Still abundant, these striking black, rust, and white eagles throw back their heads and utter loud laughing cries that can be heard for miles, one of the great sounds of wild Africa. There are few inland rivers, streams, or lakes of any size where one does not see at least a pair of Fish Eagles.

John Williams has catalogued 420 species of birds in Nakuru Park alone. This is a remarkable record for so small an area, especially when compared to Roger Tory Peterson's listing of 440 birds for the whole eastern half of North America east of the Rocky Mountains (*A Field Guide to the Birds*, 1942, 2d edition).

*... handsome Black Smith Plovers ...*

Large areas in the southern sector near Nakuru have been joined to the park recently, adding magnificent woodlands of giant yellow-barked Fever Trees. Driving through the Gothic aisles of these glorious trees, I found small birds in abundance. Several species of cuckoos, including the world's most brilliant, the Emerald Cuckoo, could be seen and heard. There are tits, shrikes, hoopoes, woodpeckers, starlings, and kingfishers. Birds range in size from the tiny Variable Sunbird to the great Verreaux's Eagle Owl.

Thanks to this park protection, mammals have increased. A few hippos still live near the freshwater springs in the lake, and the finest horned waterbuck in all Kenya graze in the open glades. I saw many reedbuck and made my only sighting, in all Africa, of the delicate Steinbok Antelope. Today, with luck, one can see Colobus Monkeys and an occasional leopard.

## *Ishasha Camp – Uganda*

In the 1960s Queen Elizabeth Park in western Uganda was a beautiful place. The 16,500-foot "Mountains of the Moon" could be seen sometimes through a broken cloud layer. The range of habitats included deep forests, grassy plains, small dramatic volcanic lakes, and two giant lakes (Edward and George), which are connected by the Kazinga Channel.

Along this channel hippos rested on sandbars, undisturbed by elephant bathing and drinking. There were waterbuck and herds of buffalo.

A large concentration of Pied Kingfishers perched by their nest holes dug deeply into the channel banks. Jewel-like, tiny Malachite Kingfishers buzzed from one reedy perch to another. Clouds of White-winged Black Terns and myriad species of water birds covered the sandbanks. Solitary Saddle-billed Storks were at secluded spots, and Marabou Storks waited beside any fisherman's dugout canoe for castaway fishheads and offal.

My favorite spot in Queen Elizabeth Park was our Ishasha camp at the park's southernmost tip. Hidden in a small forest, it was at least one mile from any passing vehicle. Perched on a low bank, it over-looked the Ishasha River. Across the river was the Congo (now Zaire). An alert birder, seated in a chair by the bank, could easily pick up 80 to 100 species of birds in a single day.

At night lions roared on both sides of the river, and twice I heard the grunts of a leopard walking the shoreline. Lying snugly in my cot, with all the tent openings carefully zipped, I felt totally secure.

Years before, on a Tanganyika hunting trip, I recall a night that was oppressively hot with little temperature change between noon and midnight. Sleeping within the confines of a tent was impossible, so I had my cot placed under a tree by the edge of a bluff, hoping to catch any passing breeze. Below me the riverbed was powdery dry, with scattered straw-colored piles of elephant dung and torn-up trenches where the great beasts had recently dug for water.

I remember lying on the cot, soaking wet, unable to sleep. Some-time about midnight a leopard, attracted by the odor of fresh meat hanging from a tree near the cooks' quarters, approached the camp. Aware of the cat's presence the camp boys heaped wood on the cooking fire and banged on pots and pans. The leopard withdrew, and all was still again. As I dozed fitfully, engulfed in the sounds of the night, I became aware of the chirping of ground squirrels and the scolding of small bush birds. I knew this meant that the leopard was returning. From midnight to dawn, almost hourly, the determined

Leopard in acacia tree

*pelican undisturbed by elephant*

leopard returned, and the din of pots and pans was repeated. Syd, camping a little distance from me, was probably sound asleep, and the camp boys accepted the cat as a routine menace.

One evening at the Ishasha camp, after watching the sunset, I went to my tent and was about to unzip the flap when I saw, coiled at my feet, directly below the lighted lantern, a deadly Green Horned Bush Viper. The colorful reptile was waiting for small grass frogs drawn to the site by insects falling from the hot lantern. I am not afraid of snakes, but I have a deep respect for them. I was debating a course of action when Syd arrived at my side. Poisonous or not, a reptile found on park land, he felt, must be protected. He resolved the problem by locating a long, pointed stick. He placed it in the center of the bush viper's coils, lifted the snake, walked to the edge of the river, and flipped the reptile across the water into the Congo.

Our usual morning beat took us over undulating grassy plains, teeming with shining Topi Antelope, elegant Kob, and buffalo. In the valley were a series of long oval mud wallows alive with hip- popotamus. Having spent their nights grazing miles from water, daylight would find them back in the protection of the water. Several hundred would mass together in the muck like beans in soup. When immersed in water these beasts are generally rather motionless. At six- to ten-minute intervals they would raise their wide, piglike heads above water to breathe, snort, twitch an ear, or defecate. The latter activity is accompanied by a rapid flapping of the tail, almost like the whirling blades of a fan. The beasts would then sink back again. Occasionally two bulls would engage in fierce battles, lunging and slashing at each other, mouths open, exposing large lethal tusks. Several hippos had enormous, deep, raw wounds on their backs. Few mammals battle more often than hippos, and it is common for death to result from such encounters.

All kinds of birds use the wide, exposed backs of hippos for a perch or feeding platform. I have photographed Egyptian Geese, Hottentot Teal, Jacanas, sandpipers, cormorants, herons, darters, and even wagtails on them, and, of course, the strange, small brown Hammer-kop Storks, who are such frequent companions of the hippo.

Hammerkop Stork ....
frequent companion of the hippo

Kob Antelope, waterbuck, and enormous monitor lizards frequented the edge of these wallows. One particular morning as many as 150 Crowned Cranes gathered by one hippo wallow. They danced and sparred with each other, flashing their large black, rust, and cream-colored wings in a choreographic study of beauty and grace.

One or two pride of lion could generally be located some miles away on the Ishasha flats. Herds of buffalo and Kob, their routine food, were always present.

One morning we watched a pride that had become separated by the river. A young male was still on one side of the 150-foot-wide stream. He sat there looking longingly at his departing companions. The scene before us filled Syd with anticipation and excitement. He had often seen a lion wade across a shallow river, but had never seen one swim in deep water.

I had my camera at hand, and, luckily, was able to record what followed. The lion tiptoed to the edge of the water, tested it with one front paw, wavered, withdrew. He repeated this maneuver several times. Finally he plunged into the stream and dog-paddled across, only his nose and half-closed eyes showing above the surface. He reached land, shook himself, then trotted after the others. Syd was to insist later he had never before seen a photograph of a swimming lion.

Not far from our riverside camp at the extreme southern tip of Queen Elizabeth Park was a warden's post. Close to the Ishasha River, it was on the eastern bank and bordered on the Congo Parc de Kivu (formerly Albert Park in the Belgian Congo). The warden was a gigantic blue-black, six-foot-six African, who would have made a perfect tackle for any professional football team. He was called Big George. Generally he manned this rondavel outpost single-handed.

Big George was a most accommodating and friendly person. We were able to persuade him to lead us into the nearby forest, frequented by chimpanzees. In his warden's uniform, barefooted, and carrying only a panga knife, Big George led us single file through the shadowy labyrinths of the woods. We followed well-worn game trails of elephant and buffalo silently for miles. The only communication between us was by hand signals. The smell of fresh dung hung in the still damp air. We heard the calls of kingfishers, touracos, and the piercing squeals of feeding elephants.

*Crowned Cranes*

Chimpanzees move through a forest either on the ground in loping gallops or, less often, swinging through the trees from branch to branch with great agility. The best chance of locating them is to look for their nests, high up in the trees. These sleeping platforms are built nightly, for the family troop moves daily in search of new feeding grounds. The newness of a nest is indicated by the condition and color of the leaves. Brown and dried leaves are old. Green but curled leaves mean the nest had probably been used within the last five days. Flat green leaves show that the nest might have been used the night before, a good sign that the animals are somewhere in the immediate vicinity.

When Big George located the chimps, we found them extremely shy. They would slink off almost immediately, swinging through the upper canopy of branches, and soon vanish from sight.

Once, amid much crashing of branches, the whole clan jumped and fell to the ground, ran, then climbed into the trees again and were gone. The dozen or so we saw were usually dark figures silhouetted against the sky.

In our search for chimps Big George led us within feet of the huge, gray rear ends and swinging tails of a group of feeding elephants. With rapid hand signals he indicated that discretion called for a hasty but quiet retreat.

On another occasion he walked us up to a group of Giant Forest Hogs wallowing in a mud hole. These African specialties were not discovered until 1904. They are the largest wild pigs in the world. They are very black, and the boars sport a large crescent-shaped swelling on their cheeks.

Big George's expertise and knowledge of animal tracking almost backfired on one occasion. Walking out of a forest, bordering on an open, grassy gully, we blindly followed him to a mountainous elephant lying on its side. He carefully studied the huge, dusty creature, then with hands over his nose indicated that the unfortunate beast was quite dead. We approached to within a hundred feet. Through my binoculars I noticed the long lashes suddenly twitch. Then a beady little eye opened. The elephant awakened from a midday sleep, rose to its feet, and shook the dust from itself. By that time we were running back to the car, not necessarily in single file, but with Big George still in the lead.

# Marsabit

My first view of 5,599-foot Marsabit and its complex of volcanic craters (in Somali called gofs) was a disappointment. Seen from a distance across the flat, rock-strewn desert floor, Marsabit rises so gradually that one is conscious only of a dark smudge on the horizon, topped by clouds. Now a National Reserve, Marsabit is located in the center of East Africa's wildest desert region. It is 340 miles north of Nairobi and 160 miles north of Isiolo.

In the 1920s Martin and Osa Johnson, as part of their never-ending search for wilderness, built a home (actually a small compound) inside a forested crater by a beautiful lake. They called it Lake Paradise. For several years they lived here, hunted, fished, photographed, and wrote. After their day the whole area was off bounds to hunters and tourists because of tribal wars and marauding Shifta natives. Only recently has this wild, inhospitable, yet fascinating region been reopened to visitors.

In 1969 my talented artist friend, Robert Verity Clem, joined me on safari with Syd. With Downey at the wheel, we drove the bleak but interesting long desert trip from Samburu to Marsabit. Arriving on the mountain, we reopened the old abandoned Martin Johnson tract to Lake Paradise. We rolled away rocks and small boulders and cleared earth slides and fallen logs. Finally the lorry with our supplies could reach the lakeshore. With a bit of searching, we found the weed-covered foundations of the Johnsons' homesite on a knoll that commanded a superb view of the crater lake. A few rusty tin cans and broken bits of china and glass were scattered about, possibly dug up by hyenas years before.

In the rapidly shrinking world of today the remoteness of Marsabit is appealing. It offers the ornithologist a wealth of specialties found nowhere else in Kenya. On the nearby valley slopes or roaming the misty moss-draped forests you could, at that time, find Ahmed, the elephant monarch of Marsabit.

In a region noted for elephants with large ivories Ahmed topped them all, with tusks weighing 140 pounds apiece (the heaviest known living ivory in East Africa). Syd and I were keen to get a glimpse of Ahmed, so we spent many days searching for him. His fame had

*Lammergeyer*

spread far and wide. Fearful of poachers, Kenya's President Kenyatta, by personal decree, proclaimed Ahmed a living national monument. During the last years of the life of this ancient giant, whenever possible guards were under orders to watch him from a distance. "Under no circumstances was he to be hunted or harassed by anyone."

Daily we roamed the hills, forests, and craters searching for Ahmed, but without luck. Park rangers admitted that they had not seen the animal for weeks.

Late afternoons we often watched for game in a long deep valley from a rocky perch on the hillside. Lilac shadows slowly crept over the boulders, bush, and grass and eventually climbed the eastern hill. Timid klipspringers would appear on rocky summits, standing tiptoe on their spool-shaped hooves while bushbuck and stately Greater Kudu, quietly browsing, slipped in and out of the dusk. The lack of lions in the area allowed the beautiful Reticulated Giraffe to feed serenely in the forests. Once, for over an hour, we watched a mother rhino and her twin calves enjoy the cool of the shade.

We walked near the dramatic cliffs of Gof Bongoli, hoping to see the Lammergeyer, but without success. This is one of the three places in Kenya where the great bearded vultures are known to nest.

When we returned to camp each day at noon, Bob Clem would take out his pad and watercolors and create a detailed impression of some bird he had seen that morning. Although hawks and eagles were probably his favorites, any bird might be his subject. I recall, in particular, his working out an exquisite sketch of a male Paradise Flycatcher perched on a mossy branch, Usnea banners and long filmy tail both being blown by the ever-present winds on the crater's rim.

A four-hour drive northward took us into the awesome Dida Galgalla Desert. Here, in this crucible of sand and heat, we hoped to see five species of birds considered rare and localized.

Carrying a picnic lunch and plenty of water and gas, we drove down from the cool wooded mountain slopes, which gradually leveled off into a sandy zone of dried riverbeds bordered by acacia trees, scattered thornbush, and an occasional desert rose. When in bloom this strange rubbery plant glowed like a red beacon in the monotone of its surroundings. Powdery dust billowed up behind the

Klipspringer

car and covered everything and everyone, entering our ears, eyes, nose, and throat. Flat black lava rocks clanked under the wheels.

The first of the five specialties we saw was a single, majestic, black-faced Heuglin's Bustard. Striding across the desert flats and scrub grass, it had the conformation and elegance of a racehorse. Motionless, its colors blended perfectly with sand, tufts of grass, and scattered bits of black lava rocks.

A few African Swallow-tailed Kites, smaller and paler than the American species, buoyantly drifted over the desert, resembling terns rather than hawks. Pale green Samoli Bee-eaters perched on the tips of isolated thornbushes. Supposedly rare, Masked Larks seemed to be everywhere, flushed by the oncoming car. Flying only a few feet ahead, they would alight near a stone or pebble and seemingly vanish, perfect in their camouflage.

The last of the desert specialties to be tracked down was a pair of Cream-colored Coursers, which we found with newly hatched

*Masked Lark*

chicks. Refusing to leave their spotted, stone-colored young, the parents stood tall together, like a matched pair of ivory carvings. All these desert birds blended so perfectly into their world that to take one's eyes off them for a moment was to lose them.

Heuglin's Bustard

I returned alone to Marsabit in 1971. Back at the forest-encircled shores of Lake Paradise the green tents of Syd's safari were a welcome sight. The tortuous track on which we had previously worked so hard was now a good trail.

Syd informed me that Ahmed had been seen recently, but no one would venture to guess where he was now. Ahmed now had two male companions, Askaris, who were never far from his side. Daily we repeated our Marsabit routine, searching for kudu (which we saw), the Gof Bongoli Lammergeyer (which we missed), and, of course, Ahmed.

On the sixth morning the boys packed up camp and were impatient to move on. Syd and I made one last tour of likely spots where Ahmed might be when we noted a ranger walking along the road. We drove up beside him, and Syd asked, in Swahili, if he knew of Ahmed's whereabouts. The ranger answered and pointed, "Yes, Ahmed is very near here."

We sped in the general direction indicated and found Ahmed and his two companions feeding quietly in bush and tall grass. We stopped about 150 feet away and watched. In slow motion the aged beast wound his trunk around clumps of grass, tore them from the ground, and placed the sheaths into his mouth. His tiny half-closed eyes, wet in the corners, were encircled by a network of countless deep wrinkles. Slowly flapping his great weathered ears, he revealed his well-known trademark — a large, wedge-shaped gap torn from the outer edge of each ear. Several times while he fed he held his head low, resting 256 pounds of stained tusks on the ground.

The light was poor, the elephant and background showed little contrast, making a bad combination for photography. I was not disappointed, for legend and nature had combined to make Ahmed a truly regal animal. It was an honor to be in his presence.

Ahmed was found dead on the forest floor by a ranger in 1974. He had died of natural causes. His estimated age was fifty-five. His hide, skeleton, and massive ivories now rest in the National Museum in Nairobi.

## Adamson and His Lions

In August, 1969, Syd, Bob Clem, and I set up camp at Meru Game Preserve. Syd was a good friend of the park director, Peter Jenkins, and Sarah, his attractive wife. They were a charming, dedicated couple, and Peter ran his 700-square-mile reserve with high intelligence and discipline. Every morning his battalion of game rangers was lined up for inspection and close order drill. Their uniforms were neat and their boots polished when they took off for their various jobs. Peter gave Syd the prime choice of campsites.

While dining with the Jenkins at their headquarters near Leopard Rock we learned that Joy and George Adamson were camped in the reserve, living separately, and working on different projects. It has long been common knowledge that both Adamsons have gone their separate ways for some time. As George put it, "There are two things in life I cannot do without: the one is gin and the other is Worcestershire sauce. Joy is not gin or Worcestershire sauce." Joy had released hand-reared cheetahs to the wilds. She was studying their behavior and writing a book about them called *The Spotted Sphinx*. George had again gone through the trauma of returning several tame lions to the wild, and he was in the throes of writing his autobiography, *Bwana Game*.

The movie company that produced the hit film *Born Free*, after completing the movie, had lost interest in the animal performers. George Adamson loathed the idea of returning the beasts to their

*ahmed*

former prison cells in various zoos. Three young male lions used in the film eventually were given to him with the idea that he would return them to the wild. George lacked females for the "pride" and accepted as a gift four five-month-old cubs — three lionesses and a male. At his camp in the park he was feeding and caring for a full complement of seven.

Having lived through the joys and frustrations of raising Elsa, and then her cubs, he had served as technical adviser for the movie. Now he found himself completely involved with a new group. Adamson was owned by the great cats to a far greater degree than he had ever owned them. They had become his whole life.

The Jenkins were upset by the project. Peter was responsible for the park's personnel and the safety of visitors. He did not like the idea of half-wild lions roaming about. He felt they would be unpredictable and therefore more dangerous than wild ones.

But Kenya owes a great debt of gratitude to the Adamsons, not only for their scientific research but for the fortune in royalties they returned to the parks and their wildlife. Feeding the lions was a major problem, for, often, Adamson had to drive a hundred miles or more to procure meat, since, of course, no hunting of any kind was allowed inside the park.

One morning while camped at Meru, Syd, Bob, and I drove several miles to Adamson's camp. His Turkana camp boy informed us the bwana was somewhere out in the bush with his lions.

George's simple camp was located at the base of a rocky hill and was encircled by a high, stout, wire fence. The Turkana explained that this was built to keep wild lions out and safely away from the tame ones. Overshadowing two wood and canvas shacks was a large acacia tree, festooned with yellow globs like straw fruit with hundreds of Black-headed Weaver Birds' nests. Within the enclosure was a wooden platform, where the lions sometimes sat or slept. Scattered about were several truck tires the lions used as toys. We left a note asking Adamson to join us at our camp next day for lunch.

Accepting our invitation, George rumbled over in his Landrover. We shared a beer or two while he and I recalled our last meeting thirteen years before at Isiolo. We were all charmed by his contagious good humor and general enthusiasm for life. He touched on fascinating experiences he had known as District Commissioner of the Northern Frontier.

The conversation somehow drifted to guns, and he regaled us with an account of his wartime days patrolling in the Northern Frontier District. While inspecting rifles at a remote outpost, he noticed one gun with its muzzle bulging out like an old-fashioned blunderbuss. When he asked how the rifle could possibly have achieved this shape, he was informed that a cleaning rod had broken off in the barrel and could not be extricated. The members of the outpost held a meeting and decided that the only way to solve the problem was to place another rifle muzzle against the blocked one and shoot it out. It was a wonder nobody was killed.

*Acacia Trees*

After lunch George asked if we would like to visit his lions in the bush. Our answer was quick and affirmative. We drove in his car because the lions were familiar with it. On our way there he suggested that in their presence we should move slowly, talk quietly, and avoid looking directly into the lions' eyes. Years of experience had taught him that a failure to observe this etiquette made lions self-conscious and edgy.

After a long drive through scrub country, rocky outcroppings, palm groves, and grassy swamps (some ringed with herds of wet black buffalo), we came upon the lions lolling in the shade. The pride had killed and eaten a giraffe that morning and were well fed and resting. As the car approached slowly, all six heads rose to study us. Ugas, a big male, blind in one eye, was still feeding on the giraffe carcass a mile or two away.

Parked beside the lions, Adamson carefully studied each in turn, to be sure that he knew them all and that no outsider had joined the group. Well off to one side, however, 150 yards away, crouching in the grass, was a heavily maned wild male. As one of the lionesses was in season, he had recently joined the pride and deeply resented our intrusion.

Adamson left the car and walked amongst the lions, gently calling each by name. Assured that all was well and that the wild male, glowering in the distance, was safely contained, he beckoned the three of us to join him. I remember walking about as if treading amid fragile china, fearful of stepping on a foot or a hidden tail. Some of the lions could be touched, while others did not trust strangers. Suki, the largest of the lionesses, rose from her grassy bed, stretched, leapt up on the hood of the car, then up on the roof, her favorite perch. One of her great forepaws dangled over the edge of the cartop. I held her paw with my hand. It felt as tough, thick, and broad as a Carolina country ham.

It was a rare and extraordinary experience to walk among a resting pride of once tame lions, now living completely on their own in the wilderness. As Peter Jenkins had asked several nights before, would that trust some day dissolve and natural savagery toward men return? Caught between two worlds, how long would they continue to remember George? When would one of them leap on to another Landrover with panicky strangers inside, thinking George was there? Some ranger, unfamiliar with the situation, could think this an unprovoked attack and shoot.

Yet George Adamson is not motivated by desire for fame or riches. He seems to crave only solitude in his Garden of Eden, working with the big cats, intent on gathering information that, in the long run, will contribute to their survival.

A tragic sequel followed only a short time after our visit to Meru Park. One of Adamson's male lions, "Boy," attacked, killed, and ate a camp helper named Stanley. The man must have misjudged the animal's attitude or disobeyed Adamson's orders. This was a shattering blow to George and threatened his lifetime of dedication, hard work, study, and understanding.

Suki on her favorite perch

# India - Tiger Hunting

THE KILLING OF TIGERS is now outlawed. Not too long ago, however, it was accepted, even acclaimed, as the exciting and glamorous sport of maharajahs, the British Raj, and visiting V.I.P.'s. To the American it brought to mind the sophisticated world traveler, the man who had been everywhere and done everything. It was the ultimate in macho sport.

In late January, 1962, Elliott Hutson, outdoorsman and good friend, left his real estate office in Charleston and joined me on a hunting trip to India. All my life I had wanted to see the wilds of the subcontinent, its animals and birdlife. Joining a hunting outfit seemed to be the only way to accomplish this. (At the time I had never heard of taking a nature tour of India.) "Tiger Camps," a Shakar firm, had been highly recommended by a Charlestonian who had been to India the previous winter. After a few routine letters with a Mr. Vivak Singh Majithia of "Tiger Camps, Ind., New Delhi," we were signed up to go.

In an early letter Majithia strongly suggested that we purchase fresh ammunition in the States and ship it well in advance to his Indian office. The local supply was old, unreliable, and often misfired in the field. On his advice I shipped a small arsenal from Abercrombie & Fitch two months ahead of time.

We left New York in a blizzard. During the flight my thoughts conjured up fanciful images from the writings of Kipling, Mukerji, and Corbett, as well as random clips from old movies like *Gunga Din* and *Lives of a Bengal Lancer*, of jeweled maharajahs living in marble palaces, Rousseau-like jungles, elephants, peacocks, and, of course, tigers.

At Heathrow we boarded another flight and continued on to Rome, Cairo, Bahrain, and New Delhi. Lack of sleep and jet lag had erased most of my exotic daydreams by the time we arrived at the New Delhi airport at 5:00 A.M. Amidst the general confusion of searching for baggage, haggling with porters, and clearing with officials we at last identified Majithia. He was a most distinguished-looking Sikh in his sixties, with piercing eyes, aquiline nose, white moustache and beard, and he wore an immaculate white turban.

Our bags loaded into a taxi, we drove through miles of squalid suburbs to reach the heart of New Delhi. I remember vividly the broad, tree-lined boulevards in the early dawn, men with stick brooms sweeping leaves in the street, the barking of dogs, the distant howl of jackals, and the pungent smell of smoke drifting in tendrils close to the ground.

Once we reached the old and elegant Claridge's Hotel, I could think only of sleep, but after no more than a catnap I heard Majithia knocking at the door and stressing the importance of obtaining

Vivak Singh Majithia

*…Swirls of Pariah Kites…*

licenses and collecting the ammunition. That first day was a nightmare of confusion, bureaucratic mismanagement, long waits in
dreary corridors for petty officials to return to their desks.

After several false leads, the ammunition was located at the Customs office. Beautifully crated and correctly labeled, the box now at
my feet could not be released until our rented guns were shown to the
officials and the serial numbers checked against Majithia's list. The
guns were at camp, many miles away, on the Nepalese border. Not
even blatant bribery could effect the release of the ammunition. Time
was short, and we left. For all I know that small, neat, very heavy box
from Abercrombie is still somewhere in Indian customs.

The next day we were driven about the city and were impressed by
the new colonial Moghul-style, red sandstone government buildings
situated in the midst of broad boulevards. The massive vice-regal
palace typified the high point of British colonialism in India. Climbing a high parapet at the Red Fort, I saw for the first time the smoky
sprawl of the Old and New cities. Whirling circles of scavenging
Pariah Kites and Egyptian Vultures seemed to be everywhere. Re-

turning to our car, we passed vendors selling marigold garlands and the usual snake charmers lying in wait for tourists, with their gourd flutes, cobra baskets, and nervously pacing mongooses.

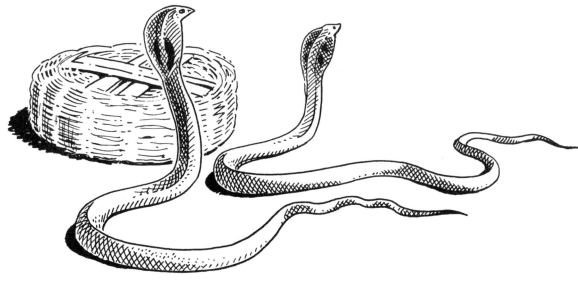

*Cobras and basket...*

Back at the Claridge Hotel, Majithia joined us for a drink. I looked forward to a long, relaxed, and, to my mind, necessary talk. We touched on several pertinent topics before I asked the question I considered most important: "At what distance does one shoot at a tiger when the animal appears?"

Majithia answered with a theatrical sweep of his hand: "Do not worry. I will present you with the tiger about here . . . ." His grand gesture covered an area that could mean anywhere from ten feet to infinity. More questions evoked equally vague answers.

Then Majithia had a burning question of his own: "Mr. Dick, is it true that Long Island is exclusively devoted to the playing of polo?" Taken aback, I answered something to the effect that Long Island is about 120 miles long and has a population of many millions, most of whom have never seen a polo field.

I am afraid that subconsciously I was comparing Majithia to Syd

Downey in East Africa. Both were products of the British colonial system. Where one was so enthusiastic and easy to communicate with, the other, Majithia, seemed disinterested, remote, almost unfriendly.

Late in the second afternoon at Delhi we boarded our jeep and headed in a northeasterly direction for the first hunting camp. Our ultimate goal was about 200 miles away, in the District of Uttar Pradesh near the present Corbett National Park and close to the Nepalese border. Once we were out of the city, with its laval flow of traffic, one town merged into the next. Darkness came early, and my first impressions of rural India were almost limited to sound and smell — odors of dust and sewage, of crowded bazaars, of dung, spices, and rotting vegetation mingled with occasional wafts of sandalwood, jasmine, and blooming citrus.   Through sporadic showers we crept along the road, our horn sounding continuously. We lurched into potholes, wove our way around buses, bullock carts, bicycles, and pedestrians, who moved only after a third blast of the horn. The most dangerous hazard was aimlessly wandering cattle. For hours we drove in the wet and dark. Some time during the night we stopped at a village, stretched our legs, bought some hard-boiled eggs, and washed them down with Indian beer. Eventually our headlights showed more greenery, and towns became fewer. Smoke from millions of dung and charcoal burners gave way to cleaner, thinner air as we climbed into the foothills.

Around 1:30 A.M. our car pulled up to the Chini rest house, situated in a dense forest of tall sal trees. Government rest houses and rentable forest lodges vary considerably. This particular one was simple, almost Spartan — a one-story cement structure divided into three rooms. There was a portable toilet, and hot and cold bath water was carried in by pail and poured into an ancient tin tub. Our sleeping bags were placed over army cots. The roof leaked badly.

Two hunting blocks, about 10×10 miles in size, had been leased for us for ten days. Both were adjacent to the rest house. The exact boundaries always remained a mystery. One block was high in neighboring hill country, and the other low along the nearby Sarda River.

The first morning at camp was glorious. The sun shone brilliantly, the air was cold and crystal clear, and the night's rain still dripped from the wet leaves. Standing on the porch of the rest house, I looked north beyond a fringe of bamboo and saw the foothills of the Himalayas, like mountains in a Chinese ink-wash scroll, marching on forever in lessening depths of blue.

We took the jeep for a general tour of the countryside. Roads were muddy, and some were quite impassable. Mysteriously and without a satisfactory explanation, Majithia decided that the mountain block was unfit to hunt — elephants slipping on steep trails, too danger-ous, and the like. We had to settle for the Sarda River.

Back at camp we met a damp, disgruntled English couple emerging from a small blue tent pitched on the lawn. They were introduced as Mr. and Mrs. Waddell. Majithia had asked them to move from the rest house to a leaking tent in order to give his new clients more room. Once we understood the situation, we rectified it at once.

As it turned out, the Waddells were part owners of Tiger Camps and wanted to join this particular hunt. Mr. Waddell was very much the British Raj type, tweedy, sporting a trim white moustache, and never parted from his pipe. He had been district police commissioner of the area for thirty-three years and a close hunting friend of the late Jim Corbett. Mrs. Waddell, the perfect female counterpart, was pretty, with pink cheeks, white hair, and lapfuls of tea cozies, which she knitted assiduously. They were a friendly couple, and we en-joyed their company very much.

Since our ammunition was of dubious age and quality, Elliott and I insisted on target practice. Also we wanted to get the feel of the unfamiliar rented guns. Majithia did not really understand why time should be wasted on such nonsense, but finally relented. We tacked a white cloth on a tree, and Elliott and I backed off about 75 paces. We fired alternately. Of the ten shots fired, three were duds. We could afford no more practice because of the shortage of shells. It was galling to remember that box we had left in New Delhi.

In this part of India tigers were hunted from a machan — a hidden platform in a tree overlooking a kill or live bait — or were driven out into the open by elephants. Small cattle or buffalo were tethered at likely places where tigers made their rounds. The baits were checked regularly. Male tigers are usually solitary animals except during mating time; only females travel with other tigers, and then generally only with their own cubs.

Driving around in our jeep in mixed forest and open grass country, we were led to three calves a mile apart, staked out as bait and tethered to a log. The first two were pathetic-looking creatures. When we located the third, we found it had been killed but uneaten. Baking in the sun, it now had the sweet heavy odor of death. I left the area depressed and strangely self-conscious.

After our first dinner at the Chini camp, we were introduced to the four elephants from whose backs we would hunt tiger. Their mahouts lined them up by the camp veranda for a customary evening snack. Their great domed heads had been blackened with the design of a jagged-edged cap, each sporting large black spit curls painted on their temples. As we handed them crude eight-pound flour cakes and blocks of raw sugar, gently swaying they lowered their long-lashed eyelids, their stomachs rumbled, and their trunks reverber-

... each sporting spit curls...

ated with pleasure; and all the while they contentedly dropped piles of dung balls. The elephants' names were Kusam, Seeta, Sitarr, and Anar. I soon became very fond of them and respected their gentleness, dignity, and long-suffering patience. It was not difficult to see how man and elephant over the centuries had developed close bonds.

The following morning, after a short jeep ride we met the four elephants saddled and waiting for us with their mahouts. The fine art of mounting an elephant had never been discussed. At a command from his mahout, each of the great beasts knelt to the ground. Walking around my assigned animal, I could not figure out whether to climb up the head or scale the side to the mattress saddle roped on the back. An elephant boy grabbed the tail, crooked it into a loop, and indicated by gesture that this was the first step up. Once I was settled on top, there was a great lurch and the elephant stood. I grabbed the mattress rope with one hand and clutched my camera, glasses, and jacket with the other. Then we were under way. I soon became used to the gentle rhythm of the elephant's pace and found it pleasant, but also discovered from this noble but swaying perch that binoculars were useless and photography impossible.

Everything on the first day's cruise was new, fascinating, and exciting. Amid a world of unfamiliar trees and other plant life we flushed Indian Peafowl and Red Jungle Fowl (the ancestor of the domestic chicken); we frightened wild pigs rooting about the edge of marshes and jumped small, chunky Hog Deer. At one point a large porcupine, disturbed in the tall grass, held my elephant at bay. At a distance I saw several handsome spotted Chital Deer. We saw signs of wild elephant, even heard them, but never actually met up with them. Of course, in my imagination man-eating tigers lurked unseen behind every bush.

It is wonderful how wide-eyed and naive one is on that first day out in entirely new surroundings. I well remember first sightings of Indian birds I had always wanted to see. The brilliant Indian Roller, Little Green Bee-eater, White-breasted Kingfishers, Blossom-headed Parakeets, and the elusive Racquet-tailed Drongos were added to my list.

From chats with Mr. Waddell, Elliott and I picked up much general information about tigers' habits, knowledge he had acquired through his friendship with Jim Corbett.

*a porcupine ... held my elephant at bay ...*

Not until many years later was I to learn that India was the last real stronghold of the tiger and that their overall numbers had diminished from perhaps 40,000 during the 1930s to 2,000 or less by 1963. Today they are battling for survival. It is appalling to read a quote by George Shaller, world authority on the Great Cats. As recently as 1965 the Maharajah of Surguja wrote to him boasting, "My total bag of tiger is only 1,150." Although man and his gun have been a serious factor to its survival, the main blame lies in the destruction of the tiger's forest habitat.

After five days of pleasant elephant rides in the wooded hill country near camp and daily checking on those gaunt, sad-faced buffalo baits, we found that none had been disturbed, clearly indicating that few, if any, tigers were about.

On the sixth morning a boy returned excitedly to camp and informed Majithia that two buffalo had been killed and partially eaten by tiger. The kills were several miles away on one of the many deltalike islands in the Sarda River. The four elephants were hurried off to a rendezvous point. Majithia, Waddell, Elliott, and I drove by

jeep and met them on a bluff overlooking the river. Once we were settled on their backs, the beasts scrambled and slid down the steep banks, then walked belly deep across the widest part of the Sarda.

Much rain had turned the swirling waters to a milky jade color. Several logs, spinning in eddies, drifted by, and I marveled at the elephants' surefootedness. We skirted sandbars and islets and eventually made our way to dry land on a large, partly forested island. Vultures roosting in a dead tree indicated the direction of one kill.

Four abreast, the elephants walked through thick, golden winter grass. Within minutes Majithia pointed down into the grass just ahead of us. Here was my first sighting of a wild tiger. My heart was in my throat as I watched the magnificent beast with the orange-and-black stripes walking sinuously ahead of the elephants. Well aware of the elephant, but not necessarily of man, the tiger showed no alarm, but walked deliberately at an even pace, not more than fifty feet ahead. Then suddenly he turned and vanished into thick bush.

We quickly broke ranks, and I was directed to a position near the shore of the island overlooking a long point of marsh grass. I was told to wait and watch.

It was a moment of supreme excitement, but now that it was here I dreaded it. In those few soul-searching minutes I knew I did not want to kill the tiger. I had allowed myself to become completely involved in the hunt, perhaps believing the confrontation would never really take place. Photographing the animal would have been more to my liking, but now it was too late. I was committed.

Trembling in anticipation, a little sick with distaste, I waited. Fasnu, my gun bearer of the day, was an ancient, distinguished Moslem, wearing a green turban, his face bristling with whiskers. He sat behind me whispering orders, not one word of which I understood.

I saw the heads of riders on elephant back approaching me, beating through the tall grass. About 80 yards ahead the grasses trembled and parted. There stood the tiger. He looked right, then left, then directly at me. Confused by the rapid instructions from Fasnu, I let the animal take three steps forward before I shot. The bullet hit the mud at the cat's feet with a splat. The tiger, in four great bounds, leapt across an exposed sandbar, gave several angry roars, and disappeared completely. Had I held my fire, the tiger undoubtedly could have been driven much closer. I felt awkward, rather foolish, but secretly pleased that it had escaped unscathed.

Daily we made the rounds of the islands on the Sarda. As the center of the river was the India-Nepal border, there were times we hunted on Nepalese soil, the arbitrary boundary line being as movable as the sandbars themselves.

Birdlife in the river area was interesting. Occasionally we saw an Osprey, but kites, especially the conspicuous brick-colored, white-headed Brahminy Kites, were numerous. Black-bellied Terns gracefully hovered over the waters looking for small fish or caught a ride on a drifting log. There were native Ruddy Shelducks, wintering Gooseanders, and small flights of tiny Cotton Teal, all white, then all dark, as they twisted and turned in flight like sandpipers.

With only a few days left before time was to expire on our leased hunting block, Majithia became edgy. We all were. Once more we took the elephants over a river crossing where sandbars were numer-

*Tiger Track*

ous. A shakari boy spotted a fresh pug mark in the damp sand. The cat must have passed by very recently, for, on close scrutiny, the edges of the tracks proved sharp, and not a grain of sand had fallen into the hollows.

The tracks led us up a steep bank. At the top we found that all signs vanished into bush and forest. Entering the cool world of shade, our elephants formed a crescent and moved forward. Sambar Deer barked, peafowl called, and off to the right cackling jungle fowl burst from cover, all signs that a tiger was near.

Elliott, on his elephant, was directed to an open marsh area beyond the forest. Before long two shots rang out, followed by fierce growls and snarls; then silence. My elephant, being closest to the rendez-vous point, moved into sunlight. There beneath me, standing on flattened grass, stood the enraged tiger. He was only a few feet away, crouched with legs apart, snarling. Then he rushed my elephant, who reared like a circus horse and bolted through the grass to open

Jungle fowl burst from cover ...

country. It was difficult for me to hang onto my gun and the mattress rope to keep from falling. I have often thought in horror of what might have happened had I fallen. Which would have been the greater danger — facing an enraged and wounded tiger or being trampled by a frightened and confused elephant? I caught a last glimpse of the tiger limping through the grass. Then he vanished into the forest.

We spent over three hours crisscrossing every section of forest and marsh, searching. Eventually we picked up a blood trail that led away from the shooting area into deep forest, only to disappear again. Reading the signs, we found that the escaping tiger, enraged with pain, had come across a Chital doe and fawn. With one slap of his great paw, he had killed the fawn and left it lying on the trail, still bleeding. Claw marks were plainly visible, but no flesh had been eaten. Quietly, the four elephants and their subdued passengers headed homeward. That evening we notified the local police at Tanakpur that a tiger had been wounded in their area and to be on guard.

*they consumed daily 600 pounds of food apiece*

The first ten-day period was over. We had to leave this lovely countryside with its forests, distant mountains, and river islands. In the jeep we drove 150 miles northwest of Tanakpur to a very different habitat.

By now it had become obvious that Majithia was not well. His increasing bad temper and acid remarks to his English partner, Waddell, had created a rift between them. The Waddells had parted company with us. We could not help noticing that Majithia constantly kept his left hand deep in his pocket. We learned later that he was trying to support an enlarged hernia, which was giving him much pain and apprehension. A proud, aloof man, with no small talk, Majithia had little capacity for casual friendship. There was no way he would allow us to share his fears or enter his private world. Tigers he could produce. He knew the best hunting blocks and had the best hunting connections. But to him this was no more than a way to make his living.

The next hunting area was in a district called Palia. Majithia owned land there called "Shirgills," which surrounded a modest farmhouse. There were vast marshes nearby, well known for their herds of Barasingha, or Swamp, Deer. Elklike, the stags sometimes grew antlers with twenty points. Vast flocks of waterfowl wintered here. Wild pig and hog deer roamed, and tigers were attracted by the local game and cattle.

We made the trip by jeep over bad roads in less than a day. The elephants and their mahouts and the accompanying elephant boys took six days. At best they could make only twenty miles a day. Every afternoon several hours had to be set aside for collecting leaves and fodder to feed these giant vegetarians. They are said to consume daily from 400 to 600 pounds of food apiece.

When the jeep pulled into the front yard of the simple concrete farmhouse, we saw that the surrounding land was flat, almost treeless, and rather bleak, a combination of cattle-grazing land and sugarcane fields.

Mrs. Majithia appeared at the door, supported by the arm of a Nepalese servant girl. She was a small elderly lady wearing a white sari, her frosted gray hair tightly pulled back into the typical large bun worn by Indian women. Her full face radiated warmth and kindness. Their son, Nivair, a man in his thirties, stood behind his mother.

... simple concrete farmhouse ...

Majithia made the introductions, then in a loud voice explained that his wife had recently suffered a stroke that had deprived her of most of her useful capacities. He as much as told us that he considered her a vegetable.

Midway through dinner Majithia announced he would depart in the morning for New Delhi on personal business and he would confirm our future flight reservations. We did not see him again until the last evening at Palia, when he returned to present his final bill.

During the ensuing twelve days we found out he had not gone to New Delhi, but had returned to our first camp, where he took on a new party of French hunters. Nivair eventually admitted this deception and seemed genuinely shocked by his father's behavior.

Elliott and I were left in the hands of Nivair. A reluctant hunter, Nivair had been placed in charge of the sugarcane crop and left to watch over his ailing mother. Mother and son were delightful people to be with, and we got along exceedingly well. High in the caste system, surrounded by numerous servants and field hands, Nivair, as a sign of rank, always dressed in a gray, pin-striped business suit with tie, black shoes, and blue turban. He gave the impression of being about to head downtown to an office. When he was in the field little changed except that his coat was replaced by a sweater.

Mrs. Majithia was extremely frail and could walk only with the help of a guide. Chatting with her at mealtime (all the family spoke British English) I soon discovered her secret weakness — Hollywood. Could I tell her about the superstars and what they were up to? Marilyn Monroe and Elizabeth Taylor were her favorites, and she devoured anything I could remember or invent about them. Seeing *Gone with the Wind* had been a high point in her life.

Our cook was a tiny man who weighed less than a hundred pounds. He produced gourmet meals, using only a frying pan and a small, portable Dutch ovenlike contraption. From these two implements emerged breads, cakes, crepes, and marvelous samosas (hot triangular fried pastries stuffed with highly seasoned meats and vegetables). Every morning he gathered or purchased his fresh curry ingredients — coriander seed, onion, garlic, ginger, pepper, chili, almonds, curry leaf, cumin seed, dhimia, turmeric, clove, and alachi. A certain amount of each was placed on a heavy wooden board and ground with an oval stone, dampened from a small silver water pitcher at hand. The game we brought back — duck, francolin, quail, hog deer, and an occasional peafowl — were prepared in an endless variety of recipes.

*Mrs Majithia was frail...*

Word traveled rapidly that there was a hunting party in the area, and soon we were told that a tiger had killed a farmer's cow not more than two miles from the house.

Our hunting gear was quickly assembled, but only one elephant, borrowed from a Majithia cousin, was available. Our four had not yet arrived from Camp No. 1. With a mahout astride the animal's hind-neck to guide the beast by prodding his ears with an ankar, Elliott, Nivair, and I headed across the open field to the kill. Hastily a

Peacock

machan was put together for Elliott in a large, dying fig tree, high above the partly eaten carcass. Here, with gun crooked in his arm, Elliott sat all afternoon awaiting the tiger's return.

After sunset, in the growing dark, and having heard no gun report, Nivair and I mounted the elephant again and proceeded toward Elliott's tree to bring him home. Nearing the fig tree, we turned on a flashlight and picked up the small red eyes of jackals feeding on the kill. Elliott was glad to leave his cramped roost, stretch his legs, smoke a cigarette, and brush the parakeet droppings from his hunting coat. Settled aboard the elephant's back, we prepared to leave. Again we shone the light in a wide curve. Approaching the tree not a hundred feet away gleamed the widely set green eyes of a tiger. But it was too late in the day to shoot. By law we were not permitted to shoot a tiger between sunset and sunrise.

Nivair had a most interesting friend and neighbor by the name of Arjan Singh, whom we called Billy. Billy was a champion weightlifter, a farmer, a keen naturalist, and an intellectual — an extraordinary combination of interests. I know he disapproved of the reason for our being in India, but he was courteous enough to hide his feelings. He talked about man-eaters in general, and his encounters with them. I recall his saying, "It is hard to explain why a tiger turns to eating human flesh. Jim Corbett suggested that this is an acquired habit rather than an innate one. The usual causes are injuries, old age, or both." Billy was the person the local authorities turned to for help when a man-eater established residence in the area.

Black Francolin

He mentioned one lame tiger that had killed six persons before he shot it. His most memorable story concerned a man who was attacked, carried for miles in the tiger's jaws, then rescued and, uniquely, lived to tell the tale. This particular man was cutting cane when a tiger, probably hunting pig, suddenly rounded a corner, grabbed the man by the waist, and made off with him. Neighboring cane cutters heard the poor man's screams. Banging on tin pans, they followed the tiger with his victim for miles. The trail of blood spots revealed that the tiger dropped the man several times, then picked him up again for a better purchase. The cane cutters narrowed the distance and finally closed in. Brandishing machetes, they forced the tiger to drop his victim. Later, in the hospital, the man well remembered his terror, the pain, the blacking out, coming to, then blacking out again; but he survived.

Years later I read that Billy had become one of India's leading conservationists. He purchased more wild land not far from the farm we had visited, close to the Nepal border. This area he calls "Tiger Haven." From here he wages his battle through articles, lectures, and photographs to save his favorite animal, the tiger. His book, *Tiger Haven*, published in 1973, is an excellent document of one man's crusade to save a bit of Indian wilderness for a nation whose disregard for wildlife is notorious.

Days passed rapidly on the Majithia farm. When not riding elephant back or on a tiger beat, Elliott and I walked the neighboring farmlands and shot quail and partridge (francolin), both the gray and the beautiful black species. One afternoon, out duck hunting in the marsh, we were standing knee deep in water. I was horrified to find my legs covered with large black leeches. Only a lighted cigarette butt would make the slimy creatures release their grip. An anticoagulant from the leeches kept the blood flowing for hours.

Every evening a fiery red sun, made even redder by the dust-filled atmosphere, settled below the horizon, and all kinds of magic night sounds encircled us at Palia. Temple bells from a distant village announced that the gods had retired for the night. Foremost from the natural world were the harsh cries of peafowl preparing to roost, followed by the gradual crescendo of a frog and toad chorus from the marshes. Jackals, on the prowl, near and far, gave vent to wild maniacal howls. On several occasions after supper, hearing the far-off rhythmic beat of a drum was reminiscent of an African tribal dance. I assumed it to be its Indian counterpart. Nivair said it was a party of local woodchoppers cutting the trees in the cool of the evening. The swing of axes was paced to the beat of a drum, and the chanting eased the monotony of the woodchoppers' tiresome chore. During the night the presence of tiger was betrayed by the distant barking of swamp deer. Tigers are great roamers and may travel ten to fifteen miles a night. Though unseen, one knew exactly which part of their range was being patrolled.

Never before had I lived for so many days in a world dominated by one word — Tiger.

Seventeen days of hunting were behind us, and only four more remained before our time expired. Once again after lunch we mounted our elephants, left the farm, and headed into the marshes. Several herds of Swamp Deer stags, loudly splashing in water ahead of us, their ivory-tipped antlers bristling above the tall grass, were wilder than usual. We moved through open wet places, clumps of twelve-foot grass, and walked past sugarcane borderlands. The elephants seemed nervous and would occasionally tremble. This edginess was quickly passed on to us.

We passed by an open grain field where a flock of peafowl were courting. Three cocks with trains fully fanned danced in tight circles about the seemingly disinterested hens. The low sun touched the birds and cast long shadows on the plowed earth.

As we moved through the marsh, my elephant repeatedly put the tip of his trunk to the matted grasses on the ground and gave hollow purring sounds. He had picked up an odor that disturbed him. Soon there was a distant garble of excited voices amid the elephant trumpeting and I heard the magic word — *tiger*! In panic a noisy group of wild pigs ran crashing through the grass toward me. I later found that

*Hunting in the marsh . . .*

Swamp Deer

Elliott, far ahead on the lead elephant, had seen a tiger that had frightened the pigs and had followed it to the edge of a wooded island.

The sun was now on the horizon, and elephants and trees became black silhouettes against a red sky. Two shots rang out. Lagging behind the lead elephant, my beast took several minutes to catch up and join the group. Nivair then raised his gun and fired blindly at likely spots to determine whether the animal was wounded or dead. If wounded, a tiger would have responded with a growl or perhaps made an attack. All was quiet. Moving forward a few feet we saw the tiger lying on its side, dead. It was a large male in prime condition. Elliott had his tiger.

Having lived, talked, and thought of little else but tiger for almost three weeks, a feeling of anticlimax seemed to affect both Elliott and me as we looked down on the handsome dead beast. The silence now gave way to a round of congratulations and handshakes, and cigarettes were passed around to the shakari boys.

The 350-pound animal was lifted to the pad on the elephant's back and secured with ropes. All four elephants ambled home in random formation. The last afterglow of sunset vanished as we arrived at the farm compound. The tiger was lifted from the elephant, and, with the help of flashlights and lanterns, it was carefully placed on the grass in a crouching position, his head resting on a small pile of bricks. This was necessary to keep the hair from creasing. A shakari boy kept an all-night vigil to make sure no animal tore the hide.

The next morning, shortly after daybreak, the skinner and his helper sharpened their knives and went to work. The inside skin was scraped of all fatty tissue, washed, and heavily salted. Carefully the skinners placed the hide, fur side down, on a bed of clean straw and stretched it into position with numerous pegs.

Word quickly passed around the locale that a tiger carcass was available at the Palia farm. Country people arrived in droves with their knives and baskets. They consider a tiger to be a walking pharmacy and every part to be highly medicinal or to have aphrodisiac properties. Later the tiger's head was boiled and the skull picked clean. The great yellow canine teeth protruded over two inches from the bone.

Skin and skull were eventually shipped to Jonas Brothers in Mt. Vernon, New York, where it was properly cured and fashioned into

... dusty vultures hissed and fought ...

that great status symbol of the time, a snarling, outstretched tiger skin rug.

With most of the flesh stripped from the headless skeleton, the remains were dragged away and left a considerable distance from the farmhouse. In a makeshift burlap blind I photographed the dusty disheveled vultures that appeared immediately on the scene. About 30 birds flapped, hissed, hopped about, and fought over the skimpy feast.

The very same day, during lunch, another excited cattle owner rushed to the house and told us that one of his finest cows had just been killed in broad daylight, and the tiger, at that very moment, was feeding on the carcass. Guns were assembled, all the elephants were made ready, and in single file we slowly plodded through dusty fields toward the dead cow. Farmers went about their chores as if nothing had happened. Looking through the grass and weed stalks, I eventually saw the white, bloated belly of the cow.

Instructed by Nivair, I moved to a given point at the edge of a field a half-mile away. I settled myself as comfortably as possible on the mattress saddle, loaded my gun, and waited. Slowly the four elephants (we had five now) walked in a wide semicircle toward me. Through binoculars I could see Elliott pointing to an object moving through the grass. With a dry mouth and pounding heart I waited.

Through the broken yellow grass I saw the tiger slowly approaching. At about 125 feet it stopped, turned broadside, raised its head in my direction, and gave me a look of imperious disdain. Aiming at mid-shoulder, I fired. The shot missed, hit the ground with a puff of dust, and the tiger, grunting, sprang to the right and ran. Instinctively I swung the gun at the moving target and fired the one remaining shot. The tiger spun in a complete somersault. The shot had pierced its heart. We waited a few moments, then dismounted and walked to where the fallen animal lay. It was a tigress. Examining her, we noticed her breasts were heavy with milk. Her glazed, open eyes increased my sense of regret. Awkwardly I leaned over and touched her head in a subconscious act to beg her forgiveness. It was probable that her cubs were hidden nearby, or, I hoped, they were already on their own, able to hunt and only occasionally nursing. I could not know. I tried to put these thoughts out of my mind.

What followed was almost a repetition of the day before — a low red sun on the western horizon, gun bearers and elephant boys lifting the animal to the back pad of the elephant, the homeward journey. The anticlimactic feeling of the day before was even more oppressive now. A sense of confused shame engulfed me. Why did I, supposedly a sensitive person, have to "prove" myself in this manner?

As the solemn procession moved toward the farmhouse, I stared at the dead tiger lying astride the elephant's back and recalled a print in a children's book on grand opera that had made an indelible impression on me — Siegfried's funeral journey — the golden blond god-hero lying outstretched on the back of a great white steed, helmeted warriors with heads down, walking alongside.

The fading, slightly torn tiger skin rug in my living room is a constant reminder of how long it sometimes takes to grow up.

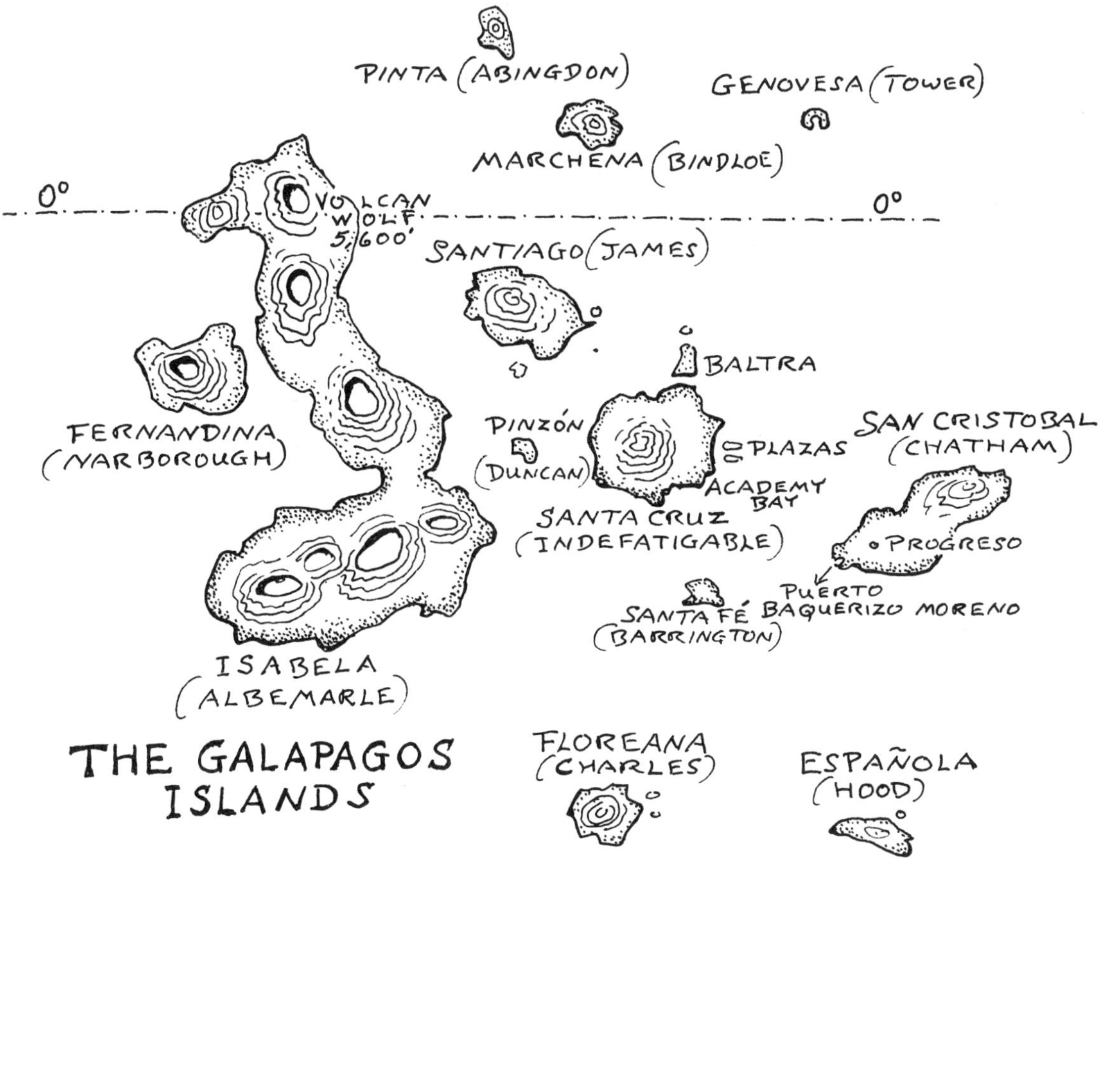

PINTA (ABINGDON)

GENOVESA (TOWER)

MARCHENA (BINDLOE)

0°                    0°

VOLCAN
WOLF
5,600'

SANTIAGO (JAMES)

BALTRA

FERNANDINA
(NARBOROUGH)

PINZÓN
(DUNCAN)

PLAZAS

ACADEMY
BAY

SAN CRISTOBAL
(CHATHAM)

PROGRESO

SANTA CRUZ
(INDEFATIGABLE)

SANTA FÉ
(BARRINGTON)

PUERTO
BAQUERIZO MORENO

ISABELA
(ALBEMARLE)

THE GALAPAGOS
ISLANDS

FLOREANA
(CHARLES)

ESPAÑOLA
(HOOD)

# Galápagos

My FIRST TRIP to the Galápagos Islands, in 1962, sounded like an ideal setup. A group of us were to sail aboard the schooner *Westward*, owned and skippered by Drayton Cochran. Aside from the obvious pleasure of the cruise, we had a mission — to bring back live specimens for the Philadelphia Zoo. There were fourteen of us on board, an assortment of ages, types, interrelationships, expectations, and, naturally, yet understandably, tensions.

*Westward* was a lovely lady, 100 feet at the waterline, steel-hulled, with spotless white sides, shining brass, teak decks, and two towering masts. Built in Germany, this was her maiden voyage, sailing westward in stages on a world-encircling trip. She now headed toward the Pacific through the Canal from Colón with her hopeful if uneasy passengers. Besides Cochran, the skipper, were his daughter Cathy and his son Charles; George F. Baker, III, his wife Kim and son Button; Brinton Coxe, a graduate engineer; Freddie Adler, a highly competent if officious TV man from Sydney; Devin Garrity, New York publishing friend; Margaret Hundley, a staff member of the Florida Audubon Society; Gertrude Legendre, an old friend and a keen outdoorswoman; myself; Lucienne, a French maid-stewardess, and Willie, our temperamental German cook.

All of us except Lucienne and Willie took a watch at the wheel, swabbed decks, and served as crew.

The three days after we navigated the Canal and left the Isthmus of Panama well behind were calm. Each day out seabirds became more numerous. On the fourth morning the highest peak of Cocos Island

*. . . Sea birds became more numerous . . .*

broke the clean sweep of the western horizon. Escorted by leaping porpoises, we entered Chatham Bay and dropped anchor at this Costa Rican island. Hillsides of dense vegetation, like a wet green sponge, spilled countless ribbons of water over cliffs into the sea.

Cocos evokes flashbacks of boobies, frigate birds, pelicans, and noddies flying about the ship, of white ethereal Fairy Terns in pairs or trios assaulting the sky, then gliding downward in dazzling aerial maneuvers. I think of our search for the four indigenous land birds of Cocos — a Cocos Finch (one of the Darwin group), a Yellow Warbler, a cuckoo, and a flycatcher; of Devin and me groping through jungle vines, lianas, and fallen Cecropia tree trunks to stumble upon an idyllic waterfall, where we stripped, sweaty and exhausted from the humidity, to stand under its cool tumbling water. Our sortie produced several Darwin Finches, a number of Yellow Warblers, but neither cuckoo nor flycatcher.

*Escorted by leaping porpoises ...*

*... Frigate birds about the ship ...*

After navigating the coast of the island in *Westward*'s speed launch, we stopped briefly at Wafer Bay, the only other safe harbor. We walked the rocky riverbed, spotted wild pigs, a handful of abandoned chickens, and one cat, and saw two deep shafts, evidence of the continuing hunt for treasure — Peruvian gold — rumored to be hidden on the island.

In today's shrinking world I wondered why an island of this size wasn't inhabited. There was no government personnel; indeed, not a soul was stationed here. Any boat landing on Cocos was supposed to obtain permission from the Costa Rican Government, but who was there to check this out? Why were there no scientists here studying this most fascinating island? I still wonder.

The 300-mile trip from Cocos to the Galápagos was distinguished only by chilling relationships among the passengers, thawed at times by meals of freshly caught dolphin and king mackerel provided by the Baker men, at other times by Gertie Legendre's exceptional talent as a social catalyst, easing tensions just by her outgoing presence, effecting truces with a soothing shaker of daiquiris.

Yet there were pleasures. With improving winds we broke out sail. Everything on board was suddenly at an unfamiliar angle. The constant throb of the diesel motors was replaced by the gentle hiss of waves lapping against the hull. Night sailing was magic — the whispering sounds of wind in the rigging, the beauty of billowed sails and the brilliant stars swinging above the mast tops, the dipper low to starboard, the Southern Cross equally low to port. These were equatorial waters. Porpoises would cut phosphorescent paths as they homed in on the bow of *Westward*.

On the evening of May 26 a long-billed, long-winged Swallow-tailed Gull swung toward us like an official welcomer. Cochran, a fine navigator, was on target. We had our first glimpse of the Galápagos Islands, described in a *Life* publication, *The Wonder of Life on Earth*; as:

Fairy Terns

"Bleak, black basaltic mountains, pitted, cratered, blistered, seamed with lava flows, littered with slag heaps, strewn with cinders, parched and prostrate beneath a sullen, smouldering sky . . . ."

Destiny has linked the names of Galápagos and Charles Darwin. In 1835, at the age of twenty-six, on the British survey vessel H.M.S. *Beagle*, Darwin paid a five-week visit to the islands.

Since youth he had been convinced that species were not unchangeable, specifically created entities, as the world then assumed, but had evolved, over many years, by the evolutionary process of natural selection. He had long searched for living proof of his theory and now had stumbled upon this living laboratory. The Galápagos provided the evidence that later produced his *Origin of Species*, a book that shook the scientific world. The drab-colored, sparrowlike finches had provided a chief clue. This family, of rather obvious common ancestry, had evolved into thirteen different species, each filling a different niche.

We dropped anchor in Chatham Island's Wreck Bay and rowed ashore to the simple dock at the town of Puerto Baquerizo Moreno, the administrative capital of the Galápagos. Longing for exercise, some of us walked the main dirt road that wound upward through a wasteland of broken black lava rock, scattered Palo Santo trees, bitter orange trees, and cactus. We passed shanty houses inhabited by dark-skinned Ecuadorians and runny-nosed children with their donkeys, cur dogs, and multicolored chickens.

Begging a ride on a passing truck, we headed five miles up the line to Progreso, formerly a penal colony. The vegetation about this small community was green with mango, guava, edible citrus, and banana trees in abundance. On an open, grassy common children were playing soccer. We continued walking upward from Progreso and passed large Miconia and Scalesia (related to sunflowers) trees festooned with banners of yellow Usnea lichen, dripping with moisture. Stubby-tailed Darwin finches of three species were everywhere, and an occasional distant pinpoint of crimson perched on a dead branch proved to be a Vermilion Flycatcher. We followed a cattle trail that led to a freshwater crater lake, but the "Garua" mist closed in, obscuring everything, so we stopped climbing and headed down the mountain into the sunshine and began the long trek back to the harbor.

*Tropic birds approached from the sea...*

The true magic of the islands was unveiled when we sailed the short twenty miles from Chatham to Hood Island. Unlike most of the other volcanic islands, Hood is a seven-mile-long upheaval of submarine lavas, unimpressive and uninhabited. But ashore it offered some of the greatest wildlife wonders on earth. Friendly sea lions swam alongside our dinghy, porpoising and barking, their shining wet heads at gunwale level only feet away. Fearless oystercatchers with their plaintive "weep-weep" calls walked on pink feet over the pitted black lava amongst scarlet rock crabs. These are nicknamed "Sally lightfoot" for their ability to run short distances over water. A Curve-billed race of mockingbirds lit on Devin's head, perhaps with hopes of finding nesting material.

Once we were ashore more mockingbirds became a minor nuisance as they examined the contents of camera bags, tugged at shoelaces, or just stood about like begging children.

Advancing up the island along a cliff edge, we failed to notice the marine iguanas until we were almost on top of them. It was the

*Waved Albatross . . . on edge of high cliffs*

scratching sounds of claws on rock that brought them to our attention. Suddenly there were hundreds of them, measuring from six inches to three feet in length, strange, dragonlike creatures with colorfully blotched red patches, a peculiarity of the Hood Island species (all others are blackish).

Cliff shelves abounded with nesting Masked Boobies (the more abundant Blue-footed species nested in the interior) and beautiful Swallow-tailed Gulls. Small parties of Red-billed Tropic Birds, mostly white with long tail streamers, approached from the sea, then disappeared into deep rock crevices where their nests were hidden. Back from the cliff edge, in the hot bushy interior, the rust-capped race of Yellow Warblers chased each other in the scrub. Stubby little Galápagos Doves with checkered wings and turquoise eye-rings walked about bobbing their heads, searching for seeds at one's feet. I stumbled on the local dark race of the Short-eared Owl, blinking at me from a fissure in the rocks. It was so "tame" I photographed it from only inches away and could have touched it.

Unquestionably the outstanding creatures on the island were the great handsome Waved Albatrosses, the largest seabird found in the eastern Pacific. Here about 10,000 pairs breed on the southern side of Hood Island, their only nesting site on earth. The surface of the island, like the tilted deck of an aircraft carrier, seems to be the only place on the Galápagos where the birds, with an eight-foot wing-span, can approach the prevailing winds and make a landing. For takeoff they must waddle up to the edge of the high southern cliffs where they can jump into the uplifting air currents. The size of a barnyard goose, these albatrosses are gentle, sad-eyed creatures with long, yellow, hooked bills, silky gold-washed heads, slate-brown backs and wings, and show fine wavy lines that run horizontally across chest and flanks. Many were incubating, each on a single white egg. Since it was early June, some were still courting, clicking bills together, bowing and cooing, an intricate display that serves to

Swallow-Tailed Gull

strengthen the bond between the breeding pair. If approached too closely, they would temporarily desert the egg, and mockingbirds would then descend from nowhere and attach the exposed egg, piercing a hole in the shell and consuming the contents.

*mangrove in the surf*

Academy Bay, at the southern end of Indefatigable Island, is the location of the Charles Darwin Research Station, flanked by native settlements and a small colony of European immigrants, many of whom have lived here since the 1930s. The staff at the Research Station showed us about the simple complex of buildings and gave us a tour of the rock-walled propagation pens for various forms of the giant tortoise that gave its name to the islands — Galápagos. Several subspecies are now on the brink of extinction, and it is hoped that young from the eleven known surviving races could be reared in captivity and eventually returned to their respective islands. However, this can happen only when they are old enough to fend for themselves and their main enemies are brought under control — the goats, pigs, and rats introduced by sailors and other visitors.

During the last century whalers stopped at the islands. The tortoises were plentiful then, and, in an age without refrigeration, they could be taken aboard and stored as a food reserve. They were put in the hold, like casks, and would live without water or food for as much as a year. Scattered records from a few available logbooks mention the removal of thousands of tortoises in a period of only a few years. Today their total population is probably less than 10,000. It was here at the station that we purchased the first of our zoo specimens: three medium-sized tortoises for the sum of three hundred dollars.

When we anchored at Academy Bay, many of the local people came aboard for a firsthand look at *Westward*. Among them were the three Angemeyer brothers — Gus, Fritz, and Karl. All were independent, rugged types with strong handshakes and open smiles. Cochran took to them immediately, as we all did, and with the greatest bit of luck he talked Karl, the friendliest of the three, into joining us for the remainder of the cruise.

Galápagos Doves

Karl, in his forties, dark and powerfully built, with a short black beard, was the prototype of all storybook sea captains. One of seven children, he had been born in Bremen, Germany. He and his brothers had all dreamed of living on a tropical island. Before the start of World War II the brothers purchased a small sailing vessel and headed for the Galápagos. A fourth brother finally left the islands, but the remaining three built homes, married, and eked out a living. They built a house for their parents and two sisters, but unfortunately they never arrived; the Angemeyer home in Bremen was bombed and the family killed, just as the war ended.

The evening before *Westward* sailed for Academy Bay the Angemeyers invited us to their house for an evening of music, song, talk, and wine. We met Karl's pleasant redheaded wife, and with Karl on guitar and Fritz on the accordion, we stumbled happily through many beer hall songs. Later we politely admired Karl's wonderfully bad oil paintings of countless crimson Galápagos sunsets. Early the following morning I rowed ashore to Angemeyer Point to photograph feeding time at their house. One German shepherd dog, two black cats, and numerous tame marine iguanas all ate canned dog food and table scraps together from a single large tin pan. The marine iguanas supposedly eat only marine vegetation, but at Angemeyer's they had adapted to man's ways. Here was a peaceable kingdom.

On a picnic excursion Devin and I joined Karl in his beat-up fishing dory, its ancient inboard motor chugging gamely but missing an occasional beat. Cruising the broken lava coastline of Indefatigable, with its scattered treelike Opuntia Cactus, we happened on numerous groups of giant Manta Rays(some weighing a ton each), which appeared as dark cloud shadows under the water's surface. Disturbed by the sound of our motor, a few would leap into the air like huge bats, soar briefly, then splash back into the sea.

We approached the narrows that opened into Turtle Bay, our destination on Indefatigable Island, and saw large swells, indicating a shallow coastal reef. Karl studied the wave action carefully while he figured our safest entrance point. Then he headed us for the calm inner waters. Once past the reef, I looked over my shoulder and saw a monstrous comber curling behind us, the type that sometimes reappears in my dreams, traveling at our speed, gaining a little, about to break, yet not quite. Angemeyer's expert seamanship had led him to

*... giant Manta Rays leapt ... like huge bats*

the only possible entrance point, a narrow gap with twenty-foot waves breaking on either side of his small boat. Later we were informed that only days before a group of Norwegian sailors had capsized here with all lives lost.

Karl had brought along an Academy Bay neighbor, Robert McGough. The young man was suffering from amoebic dysentery and had the emaciated look of a Dachau survivor. Relaxed by a rum drink or two, trembling with fever, he told us his story. He and his family were the sole remnants of a group of a hundred American families originating in Seattle. In 1959 they had put up $2,500 per family for transportation and establishment in the Galápagos. They had been promised an island paradise where they could be self-sufficient, free from the worries of civilization. Once at the dock at Wreck Bay, however, they were dumped ashore with all their possessions. The promoter collected his money and vanished. Most of the families struggled for a short time to eke out an existence. Karl

*Karl and Land Iguana*

observed that the women proved practical, industrious, and hard-working, while their men were mostly impractical dreamers. Soon all returned to the States, except the McGoughs. Robert subsisted on Angemeyer's generosity and scant pay as a fisherman's helper.

Cochran's *Westward* took us next to the Plazas, small twin islands just off the eastern coast of Indefatigable. Approaching the low western shoreline of one of these mile-long islands, we were escorted by herds of playful young sea lions. On the beach the bulls roared among their harems, who rested about the rocks like great clumps of sausages. Hardly were we ashore before Karl captured a large, golden rust-colored land iguana he spied scurrying about in the low sesuvium growth covering the ground. He grabbed it by the tail as it retreated down a hole under a rock and, applying a steady pressure, eventually pulled it free.

Eleven years later I returned to this same island. The beautiful sesuvium ground cover, once the color of autumn leaves, was mostly gone. The feet of tourists had trampled the root systems and pulled the plants apart. The once shy golden dragon iguanas were now as tame as house pets waiting for handouts of sandwiches and fruits. Having given up the normal territorial life and diet of cactus leaves, they appeared battle-scarred and diseased. I gather, too, that they were no longer breeding.

Under Angemeyer's guidance we dropped anchor at various sheltered coves, swam in shark-free bays, where the Humboldt Current kept the water at a comfortable 65 degrees. We climbed volcanic hills, where basaltic lava flows swirled down to the sea like hardened chocolate syrup. Angemeyer took us to a hidden cove on James Island, and we snorkeled and swam with fur seals, now staging a slow comeback from near extinction. Karl knew the right holes in several bays where grouper gathered, and soon the ship's freezer was filled. He took us to a vast mangrove lagoon, where we spotted a Great Egret and an Osprey, both uncommon visitors to the Galápagos, and then on to several hidden circular volcanic lakes to see flamingos. He knew a pass between shoals of mangrove where Green Turtles gathered by the score. Cochran and Button Baker, armed with rifles, shot two of them when they surfaced. They were hauled on deck and butchered for food. Margaret Hundley, an arch conservationist, was shocked by the bloody operation and vanished

... we dropped anchor in a sheltered cove...

*black marine Iguanas ... Point Espinosa*

into her cabin for two days, refusing to eat. I understood her depression, but admit to enjoying the thinly cut, breaded turtle steaks. The turtle soup, gray-green, thick, and gelatinous, spiked by generous amounts of Madeira, was delicious, a rare treat.

We sailed around the northern coast of Albemarle, the largest of the Galápagos Islands, and beheld Volcan Wolf, its highest peak, soaring 5,100 feet above sea level. Albemarle stretches seventy miles and has six large volcanic calderas with over 2,500 smaller cones in evidence. We dropped anchor at the straits between Albemarle and Narborough Island at a spot called Point Espinosa. This is the most spectacularly scenic area in the entire archipelago. The point is attached to Narborough Island, the only large island remaining an untouched sanctuary, where man has never settled nor released his destructive companions — dogs, pigs, and goats.

The black ledges and rocks of Point Espinosa swarm with wildlife — seals, cormorants, penguins, and thousands of the prehistoric-looking black marine iguanas. Captain Fitz-Roy of the *Beagle* described his first sighting of this spot as "a fit shore for pandemonium."

With our three tortoises, three land iguanas, and eight marine iguanas on board, as well as three snakes overtaken by Charlie and Cathy Cochran on James Island, we went after the last wildlife specimens for the Philadelphia Zoo. Karl, using a large fishnet, had no trouble scooping up a family trio of Galápagos Penguins preening on a rock. Soon after, he captured a pair of Flightless Cormorants. The penguins, as expected, were enormously appealing. But the two Cormorants, turned loose on the hot deck, appeared pathetic and out of place. They are large, dark, reptilian birds with milky-blue eyes, furlike plumage, and enormous feet. I saw little hope for them as an attraction in a zoo. Extremely rare, there are fewer than eight hundred pairs in existence. Over the many centuries of evolution, flying less and less, their wings have shrunk to the size of tags. Margaret Hundley and I took a strong stand on their behalf. We realized that the zoo wanted them mainly as a status symbol, a

... Flightless Cormorant ...

"first," since no other zoo in America owned a pair. In captivity we felt they would be more ridiculed than admired. After a lengthy argument with the skipper, Cochran relented, and the serpentine creatures were slipped overboard at Tagus Cove a few miles from the place where they had been captured.

Of all my trips this one to the Galápagos took me farthest back in time, where in remote pockets nature was least affected by man. Perhaps nowhere else on earth are wild creatures so completely unafraid of man. Today thousands of picture-taking, peering tourists visit the Galápagos annually at some risk to the island's fragile ecology. Perhaps the islands are being loved to death.

Stricter rules are now in effect, and ways are being sought whereby man can live on or visit these islands without destroying them. With a different approach, the terrible mistakes made in the past may be avoided.

Galápagos

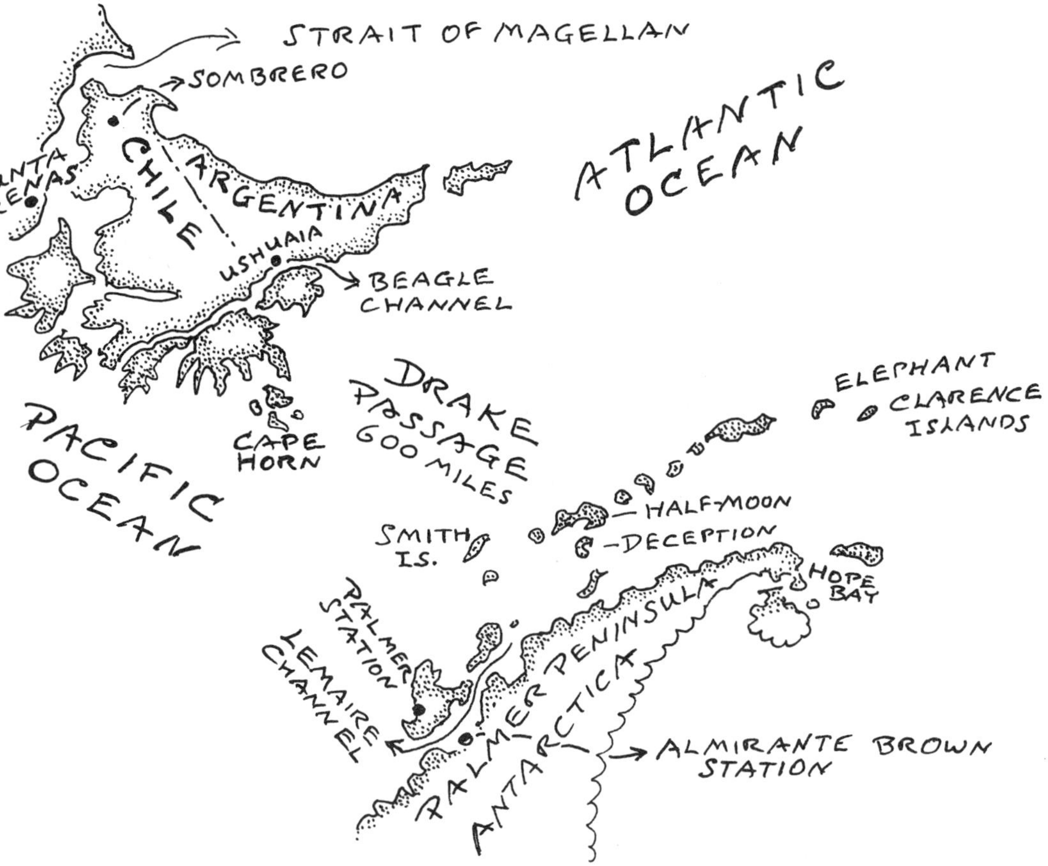

STRAIT OF MAGELLAN

SOMBRERO

ATLANTIC OCEAN

PUNTA ARENAS

CHILE

ARGENTINA

USHUAIA

BEAGLE CHANNEL

DRAKE PASSAGE 600 MILES

PACIFIC OCEAN

CAPE HORN

SMITH IS.

HALF-MOON

DECEPTION

ELEPHANT

CLARENCE ISLANDS

PALMER STATION

LEMAIRE CHANNEL

PALMER PENINSULA

ANTARCTICA

HOPE BAY

ALMIRANTE BROWN STATION

# First View of Antarctica

A LOW-KEYED TRAVEL advertisement in a 1965 issue of *Natural History* magazine invited tourists to behold for the first time the magic of Antarctica. I had always longed to see a Wandering Albatross. Devin Garrity, always a good traveling companion, volunteered to accompany me.

Lars Eric Lindblad, organizer of the Lindblad Travel Company, arranged with the Argentine Navy for a ship that could transport tourists in moderate comfort to the earth's least-explored and exploited continent. The experience was mind-boggling and in a personal way profoundly moving. A sudden storm, a broken landing craft, a fortuitous shelter, and a successful rescue operation provided extra dividends that neither Lindblad nor the Argentine Navy had anticipated.

In January, 1966, we met our fellow travelers, about fifty of them, in Buenos Aires. Lars Lindblad led our group. He is a vivacious, rather big but agile man, heavy-lipped, and with a bang of hair over his brow, the epitome of a Norseman. We passengers were a rather mixed bag. Our ages averaged about fifty to sixty-five. Most of the party had traveled extensively. Antarctica was their last frontier. There were single, retired businessmen, traveling couples, and schoolteachers in pairs. We had with us the man who invented the popular game of Monopoly, and a chemist who was responsible for Rolaids. Both would spend much of their time comparing royalties. "Mr. Rolaids" admitted that he annually took a one-month trip by himself. Any place in the world would do. We would meet on deck in the mornings and he would say, "Hope the birding is good." I would answer by listing the birds I had recently seen. "Please don't tell me what they are; they're all the same to me. I just hope you are enjoying yourself."

There was also a young American girl on a Fulbright scholarship studying "the social implications of the Argentine tango." There was a socialite couple from the Middle West and a distinguished-looking Anglo-Argentinian who never left the bar stool, even to walk out on deck. As he said to me at the end of the trip, "When I return to my club in Buenos Aires, I will have been its only member to have seen the Antarctic." Lindblad was determined that the trip would be interesting, educational, and enjoyable.

... noble hulks and masts
      at Punta Arenas ...

*... sculpted by the constant winds ...*

We flew south from Buenos Aires over the Patagonian pampas country, which appeared dry and monotonous. Yet I was fascinated by the star-shaped designs made by trails of cattle and sheep walking to and from water holes. The rugged, snow-capped spine of the Andes appeared off to the west when we approached Punta Arenas. These imposing mountains are on the northern, Chilean side of the Strait of Magellan.

After clearing customs, we settled in the town's ultramodern hotel, which faces a small city park with an heroic bronze statue of Magellan. Opulent Victorian houses, built with wealth derived from mining and ranching, bordered this park. Their elegance quickly gave way to the unabashed squalor of rusting, tin-roofed houses and shacks that housed some 25,000 other people. Walking to the city dock, one became aware of rugged mountain peaks connected by swags of snow and blue glaciers, an imposing backdrop for the cold, dark, white-capped waters of the Strait.

Black-browed Albatrosses, Shearwaters, and Giant Petrels skimmed the choppy seas on stiff wings. Magellanic Penguins in close schools porpoised like tuna and vanished under the waters only to reappear shortly. I was thrilled to see flocks of the large Crested Duck, the sunlight accentuating brilliant purple speculum patches. There were also groups of Brown Pintail, very chunky Flightless Steamer Ducks, and lovely Kelp Geese on shore or swimming along the coast. King Shags, a type of cormorant, battled strong headwinds, while Dolphin, Kelp Gulls, and Arctic Terns cruised the water's edge for food.

Many noble hulks and masts from great, square-rigged sailing ships, now stranded and forgotten, rested at stark angles along the shoreline at Punta Arenas, time and weather forever attaching their bones.

It was midsummer in this part of the world. The roadside and sheep pastures were peppered with wildflowers, the most conspicuous being drifts of white daisies. Wild fuchsia bushes in hedgerows

Rhea .... wandering alone ...

*... large Crested Caracara ...*

and drifts with their red-and-purple hanging blossoms seemed to be everywhere. Although much of the forest land had been cleared for grazing, the higher slopes were thickly covered with small-leafed members of the beech family. Those in clumps or standing singly in the open were wonderfully sculpted by the constant winds and supported long banners of yellow Usnea moss. Fences were little more than crude piles of weathered beechtree stumps interlocked together. Rocks, wood, or fencing all resembled Fauvist paintings, spotted and blotched with brilliant-colored lichens.

Nearby in the flat pampas country, flocks of Magellan Geese flew about or grazed in the sheep range. Far off on the horizon I saw a Darwin's Rhea, the South American cousin of the ostrich, wandering alone, a solitary figure in an empty land. Numerous varicolored plants hugged the ground. Some were in bloom and others carried berries, the whole spreading like an endless Persian carpet.

Cayenne Lapwings, which are large-crested plovers, almost always in pairs, ran in short spurts and called constantly as they led us away from their hidden young. Both the large Crested Caracara and the smaller brown Carancho Caracara were common and often perched on telephone poles.

Near the roadside I recall spotting a cluster of windblown feathers emanating from one place. My glasses revealed a Peregrine Falcon feeding on a domestic pigeon. Even as I approached, it refused to relinquish its prey. I got to within a hundred feet before the falcon flew off.

From Punta Arenas, which is in Chile, we traveled to Ushuaia, Argentina, the southernmost city in the world, at latitude 55 degrees South on the Beagle Channel, and our port of departure. This is a distance of 150 miles as the crow flies, but in fact is much longer and more complicated. The trip involved a short flight over the Strait to Isla Grande in Tierra del Fuego, then three bus trips with two breakdowns. We broke an axle on the open plain near the oil town of Sombrero. When we at last reached this community, we were fed and bedded for the night in a makeshift dormitory. An American oil company, hoping to make life more enticing for its employees and families, had built a model residential complex with a handsome nonsectarian church, a movie house, and a large greenhouse filled with tropical plants and trees, garden pools, walks, and resting benches. Flanking the greenhouse was a superb modern gymnasium with an Olympic-size swimming pool. Outside this glass-enclosed utopian world a cold wind howled constantly over the treeless plain.

After another breakdown and a second night's delay, we finally headed down to Ushuaia. As we entered dense beech forests, small flocks of olive-green Austral Parrots (the southernmost species) flew screeching across the road and vanished. Descending the mountains through patches of misty clouds and driving past torrential streams, we had our first glimpse of Ushuaia and the Beagle Channel far below us. A beautiful setting for what was then a not-so-beautiful town.

At the docks, nesting beside two British freighters, was our Argentine navy transport, A.R.A. *Lapataia*, 68,000 tons, 300 feet long, painted black, and with a gloomy dark-gray superstucture. *Lapataia*, now operating as a tourist ship into Antarctic waters, was the instrument of a goodwill experiment by the Argentine government. She carried a complement of 125 crew, some navy wives, and was expecting fifty tourists.

After a quick inspection tour, we realized that the *Lapataia* would never compete with the *Ile de France*. Devin and I, perhaps the two largest men on board, found our stern cabin hardly larger than a train roomette. We could scarcely turn around in it, let alone change clothing — one of us would have to step outside. Hot water for showers was available only between 7:30 and 8:00 A.M. Except for a good ship's baker, the food was generally poor, heavy on starches and lacking green vegetables. The bar was a festive spot, in the beginning, but in rapid succession it ran out of tomato juice, soda, tonic water, and, finally, beer. Fortunately, the Argentine wines served at meals were in ample supply and excellent.

The first morning at sea sirens blew and we were all summoned to the main saloon for lifeboat drill. We were given a lecture on sea survival, safety precautions, and what to do in case of fire on board. We were then handed orange-red life jackets with a whistle and flashlight attached. In English and Spanish instructions were given on what to do while floating in the water. We were then told that survival in Antarctic waters could be no longer than a few minutes at most. This brought a nervous laugh from everyone, and the subject was never mentioned again.

Antarctica, bigger than the United States plus Mexico, has been a continent with little history, few people, and, away from the coast, little life. Yet an extraordinary paradox exists, for this continent is ringed by the world's richest and liveliest ocean. Many offshore islands are crowded with seals, birds, some insects, and a few plant species. This peripheral ring of animal life is due to an unusual mixing zone called the Antarctic Convergence, located mostly between 50 degrees and 60 degrees South latitude, though it varies in width and location. Nutrient-rich, relatively warmer waters well up from the deeper regions and merge here with the cold Antarctic surface waters. This provides a perfect climate for an explosion of phytoplankton and zooplankton. These single-celled organisms feed larger, more complex forms, including small crabs, krill, shrimp, and so on up the biological ladder to the great Blue Whale. This ultimate creature, the largest in the world, may swallow tons of krill in a very short time. The Convergence is a bountiful supplier of food for penguins, petrels, albatrosses, cormorants, gulls, seals, elephant seals, fish, and whales.

The Antarctic continent itself claims the world's strongest winds and coldest temperatures. It is also the world's highest continent, with an average height of 6,000 feet. Should this great ice cap, now held in place by mountain ranges, melt, the oceans of the world would rise 200 feet. The germ-free, sterile air and the intense cold preserve materials almost indefinitely. A discarded cigarette, an orange peel, or a beer can tossed on the ice may remain for centuries, or until the ice mass slowly makes its way into more northern open ocean.

During the International Geophysical Year of July, 1957 to December, 1958 more than forty stations were established in Antarctica. Today there are over seventy. The claims and rights of the twelve nations involved have been temporarily settled by treaty.

The Drake Passage, stretching from Cape Horn to the Antarctic Peninsula, is 600 miles of the world's roughest and most unpredictable sea. The first day out, with a slight following breeze, *Lapataia* moved over almost flat waters. On the stern deck I watched Giant Petrels (called "stinkers" from whaling days) glide effortlessly behind the ship waiting for the garbage dumped overboard periodically. Kelp Gulls, Black-browed Albatross, tiny Wilson's Petrels, and the pigeon-size, boldly-checkered Pintado Petrel were almost always visible.

On the second day at sea, as we approached the "Shrieking 60's," the weather changed. A cold gray layer of clouds hung over the ocean. Small bergs and ice floes began to appear. Lovely, delicate blue-gray prions (another Antarctic petrel), with a black letter "W" sketched across both wings, now followed the ship regularly. Seemingly from nowhere appeared the king of all seabirds, the hero of Coleridge's *Rhyme of the Ancient Mariner*, the supreme master of flight, whose wings may span over twelve feet — the great Wandering Albatross.

Far astern it crossed the boiling wake and within seconds was only a few feet off the lee side of the ship. Making a steep bank, it vanished in the trough of a wave only to reappear again. Its flight pattern described a two-mile-long figure eight, and its body and wings formed a great white cross against the dark waters. There is a rare grandeur in its flight, effortless grace, a sense of independent freedom in an otherwise empty world. At this moment themes from

... the great
Wandering Albatross

Gustav Mahler's Seventh Symphony coursed through my mind's ear and complemented the ever-restless immensity of this the most dramatic and loneliest of seas.

We approached Smith Island, the southernmost of the South Shetland group, which lies west of the Antarctic Peninsula. Here the mood of Antarctica crept into the marrow of one's bones. Rising almost 3,000 feet out of the dark seawater, this ghostly configuration of ice and snow-covered rock towered above flat floes and an endless variety of oddly shaped icebergs. The big bergs are truly majestic, even though most of their bulk is hidden beneath the surface. They move with the currents, seemingly unaffected by crashing waves, floating ever onward with solemn dignity. Close to, the thunderous booming of seas attacking their peripheral ice caves is a memorable sound.

We cruised the western coast of the Antarctic Peninsula and entered a spectacular harbor at Melchior's Island. The temperature was in the high twenties, not as cold as I would have expected it to be.

In the evening we anchored in this fjordlike cove encircled by high walls of white snow, sapphire ice caves, and blue-gray waters under leaden skies. In this part of the world, despite overcasts there is always a narrow band of yellow sky along the horizon, be it midnight or noon. This phenomenon has yet to be explained to me. An overpowering curtain of muffled silence surrounded us. When one left the overheated smoky lounge to go on deck, the air struck one's lungs like menthol. Tiny Storm Petrels, like black butterflies, danced and skipped over the cold water; and dark-brown Skuas and Kelp Gulls on silent wings would glide past to settle on nearby ice floes. Talking to a companion, words sounded foolish.

The next morning, dressed in our orange-red parkas (this color proved the most visible under polar conditions), we were herded into a surplus U.S. Navy landing craft and taken ashore. The site was near an abandoned Argentine scientific station. As this was our first landing on the southern white continent, Lars Lindblad brought along several bottles of champagne. They needed no ice for chilling. Standing on a hillside with paper cups, we toasted each other, Argentina, and the Antarctic.

The *Lapataia* then hoisted anchor and moved a few miles on to an active station called Almirante Brown, named for the Irishman who

*Almirante Brown*

founded the Argentine Navy. Argentina's most important scientific station consisted of a small cluster of metal and wooden shacks perched above the sea on a rocky shelf, directly below 300 feet of an exposed rock pinnacle. All about us, dwarfing boat, buildings, and people, were ever-present white mountains.

The commandant asked those of us who wished to climb the pinnacle to avoid stepping on the clumps of green pillow moss that grew in crevices on the sheltered side of the hill. These mosses, along with lichens and two flowering plants, comprise the entire list of Antarctic vegetation. The moss, frozen most of the year, has a very brief burst of life when it thaws under the direct rays of the sun. Not every year provides a thaw, though. A few of us climbed the pinnacle and were careful to avoid disturbing these great, velvety-green pillows.

Ten years later Keith Shackleton and I climbed this same pinnacle. We found little moss left. It had been carelessly trampled on by subsequent visitors, and was cluttered with glass and beverage cans.

Blue-eyed Cormorants, the only members of that family to breed on the fringes of the continent, nested at the base of the pinnacle, but were impossible to approach. At the boat landing Sheathbills walked about the rocks like so many white pigeons. These strange birds are a family by themselves, and taxonomists place them somewhere between shorebirds and gulls. They live among colonies of seals and penguins, tiptoeing among the latter, feeding on almost any form of marine life, birds' eggs, or chicks, even seal excrement.

Massed bergs and ice floes turned us away from the spectacular Le Maire Channel, a dramatic mountainous pass between the mainland archipelago and a series of westward islands. Seals floated on flat floes like so many scattered sausages among clusters of dozing penguins, who stood, or lay, on their white bellies.

the Lapataia ...

Pintado Petrels

We visited Palmer Station, an important American scientific outpost. It was gratifying to find the personnel to be such interesting
men. Sporting heavy beards, they seemed genuinely glad to see us.
They had much to say about their projects, most of which were of a
highly technical nature — atmospheric carbon monoxide concentra-
tions over the South Pacific (Stanford University); anatomical inves-
tigation of Weddell Seals (Harvard University); dreaming and wak-
ing patterns of station personnel (University of Oklahoma). They had
an ample supply of movies, taped music, and good food. Sunday
services were conducted in a room with walls covered with full-
length, buxom pinup girls. Good humor was exemplified by a sign
tacked on a door: "Housemaid wanted — Inquire within."

*nesting Adelies....*

We were taken by boat to a nearby Adelie Penguin colony. These birds are the smallest and most numerous of all Antarctic penguins. They are the familiar "formal evening dress" birds so often seen in cartoons. The late February nesting season was nearing its end. Slippery mud-and-snow slush was bright pink with the krill digested by these birds and deposited as excrement. The odor of ammonia was unpleasantly strong.

The penguin chicks were almost grown and looked messy and disheveled, being at that awkward mottled stage between fluffy down and feathers. They huddled close together in groups called crèches of from twenty-five to several hundred. This afforded them mutual protection from the ever-present danger of predation by Skuas. A weakling or stray is likely attacked, pecked to death, and eaten.

Finding myself surrounded by penguins, I tried not to become too anthropomorphic about them, but it was difficult. Their humanlike stance, gestures, and highly expressive eyes force one against one's will to think of them as small people wearing tuxedos. Adelies, like several other penguin species, have a delightful way of handling what must be their most precious possessions, a handful of nest pebbles. There is a formal presentation and delivery, with much wing flapping, head stretching, vocal braying, and bowing. This ritual seems to be a means of mate identification, as the sexes are seemingly unidentifiable. Neighboring birds consider it great sport to steal a pebble or two when the owner is preoccupied.

At Palmer Station the Adelie colony parents are generally only a short distance from food in the open sea. Some Adelies live closer to the pole, but winter at sea. When spring returns, in October, they may walk and toboggan on their bellies as far as sixty miles or more over solid ice and snow to return to their original nests. Two eggs are usual for each nest. For about two weeks the male incubates the eggs in a pouch between his legs. He then changes place with the female. Having been foodless for perhaps more than a month, the male then hurries to the sea for sustenance. In summer, when the ice pack is broken, the long trip to open water is shortened considerably. Stuffed with semidigested krill, the male then returns to his waiting mate and the new, hungry chicks.

Leaving Palmer Station, we slipped through Neptune's Bellows, a narrow broken gap in the rim of a great flooded crater centered on Deception Island. Discovered in 1820 by Captain Palmer, this is probably the best-known island in Antarctica, having been used as a whaling port and a safe harbor. Hill slopes of volcanic ash, dusted with snow, surround the circular bay. Only a few months after our 1966 visit the island rumbled into activity. Dust and ash rose several thousand feet into the atmosphere, and a new island 3,000 feet long appeared in the crater harbor.

Gale winds kept us from dropping anchor, and for two days we circled the bay in Deception Island. On the third morning the winds abated, and we went ashore in the landing craft. The black lava beaches had a band of live krill several feet back from the high-water mark. Like wriggling bits of broken pink glass, tons of these creatures lay dying, unable to return to sea. The storm and tide had apparently washed them ashore. Back from the beach bubbling fumaroles of steam blew white clouds into the cold air. Two hardy crew members actually bathed in one of these volcanic spas.

A few of us were guided over the volcano's rim to the great basalt dust flows that slope to the sea on the other coast of Deception Island. It was difficult to walk on the steep, slipping hillsides.

On the flat lava rock apron near the shore a colony of about 5,000 Chin-strap Penguins, all braying loudly, were ending their nesting cycle. These are stylish birds, black-and-white with a narrow black band under the chin, similar to the angled strap that supports a military shako. Single birds slowly waddled down to the water, holding their flippers outstretched for balance while hundreds returned to shore in leaping schools, laden with krill to feed their well-grown hungry young.

At Half-moon Bay, in the South Shetland Island, an all-white mountain, bright by moonlight, rose behind the small, unused scien-

Half-moon Bay

*...the landing craft...*

tific station of Teniente Camara. From the deck of the *Lapataia* it seemed no larger than a matchbox.

After breakfast the next morning the landing craft took some of us ashore, making two trips. Devin and I were in the first boatload. The seas were glassy calm and the sky heavily overcast. Ashore we walked over crunching gray pebble beaches and slipped on rocks green with algae. Blue-eyed Cormorants, Kelp Gulls, and Sheathbills posed on odd-shaped boulders and chimneylike pinnacles encrusted with brilliant yellow, rust, and black lichen. Young Weddell Seal pups lay half asleep and seemed to enjoy having their bellies scratched. And several nonbreeding Gentoo and Chin-strap Pen-

*Chin-strap Penguins on Deception ...*

guins stood about idly, undisturbed by the red-jacketed humans invading their world. Random piles of bleached whalebones turned gray in the falling snow.

By ten o'clock the landing craft loomed into view, pushed her bow up on shore, and returned the first group to the *Lapataia*. The winds slowly increased. Although I was well clad, knife-sharp gusts crept down my collar and up my wrists. A few of us, still ashore, walked about for an hour before the boat returned for its final trip. Snow fell heavily when the craft beached, and crewmen held out hands as we slipped and shuffled up the ice-covered ramp. We were all looking forward to the warmth of the *Lapataia* as the bow door was pulled up and closed. The ensign on the wheel reversed the motor to pull away from shore. Calmness had turned to rage as eight-foot waves, now driven by a gale, pounded the angular craft's stern and high, upright sides. Time and again, with the grinding sound of propeller spinning on stone, the helmsman tried to pull the craft into deep water, but the winds pushed us back against the beach. Blue water started pouring over the portside gunwales, soaking all aboard.

The young ensign in charge realized that the situation was now beyond his control. He dropped the bow door and we all jumped knee deep into the icy water and waded ashore. Like red-jacketed penguins we were a confused, disgruntled group as twenty of us filed up the hill to the abandoned shack that we had seen the night before. With a seventy-mile-an-hour gale pelting snow at our backs, we forced open the door. Four small windows gave little light. We groped about, and by the dim glow of a cigarette lighter discovered the hut consisted of five rooms. To the right, nearest the broken-in door, there was a small, partitioned kitchen fitted out with an old, pot-bellied stove, several wooden chairs, and shelves with a kettle, cups, plates, and some cooking utensils. A large closet was supplied with stacked blankets, canned foods, a tin of tea, matches, candles, and two full bottles of cognac.

Our prospects were bleak. We were grateful for shelter, but the temperature in the hut was well below freezing. The small stove could heat only a limited area, even if fuel were located. Our spirits were further dampened when the crew members, including the young ensign, returned from a fruitless struggle with the beached landing craft. Her metal plate sides had buckled, and there was no way to save the engine. The crew was drenched, and their clothing was glazed with ice. It was plain that the ensign was suffering from shock and exposure. Two of the crew, raised in northern Argentina and unaccustomed to the cold, were weeping from fear and pain.

For the first two hours there was no one in charge, and we wandered about in complete confusion. Then two Argentine ladies, Graciela, the wife of Admiral Varela (head of the Argentine Navy), and the Admiral's sister, Josefina, a biologist, assumed leadership. With quiet authority they began by telling us what to do and helping us do it. I was surprised to learn that these two attractive, dark-haired ladies were both actively involved with the Antarctic Institute in Buenos Aires. They had been with us for the entire trip, yet had remained very much to themselves.

Spotting the stove, Graciela asked a group of us to go outside and search for coal. She was sure there would be a supply close at hand. Near the front door we did find, hidden under the snow, a pile of coal. We started a fire with wood from a broken crate, added coal, and eventually were rewarded with a warm glow. Next we melted snow in the kettle to provide hot water for tea. The needy were taken care of first. Some were handling their fears better than others, but eventually all thirty of us, twenty passengers and ten crew, had our turn at a cup of tea. The sailors were massaged to relieve agonizing cramps, given brandy, and wrapped in dry blankets. Laundry lines were strung up near the stove, and we tried to dry the wettest clothing. One elderly couple, quiet and noncomplaining, were bedded down on cots and soon appeared to be sleeping.

A sense of growing camaraderie developed as we huddled in the living room of this makeshift shelter earlier abandoned by unknown scientists. We laughed and told jokes, sang songs, and played games with a pack of fifty cards. The first flush of excitement wore thin. Our cigarettes ran out. The numbing cold got worse. We knew we were in trouble, still fearful, wet, dependent on a small stove that gave only limited heat to one small room. The walkie-talkie had been overused during the confusion and was now dead. Communication with the *Lapataia* had ceased.

One of the two brandy bottles disappeared. We found it later and discovered it had been completely drained by one of our fellow passengers. Unable to cope, and in a state of morose inebriation, he huddled miserably in his Brooks Brothers overcoat. His wet oxfords stretched toward the stove, he stared at the floor, refusing to communicate with anyone. He seemed to want nothing more than to die.

A chubby country club aficionado, who could drop status golf courses faster than I could name birds, made loud criticisms about inefficiency and lack of leadership. He made colorful threats of reprisals when rescue came. A sharp verbal thrashing from a retired navy officer, Captain MacDonald, finally subdued him.

But a young Lindblad courier and cruise director was most worried about his paying clientele. He buttonholed the Argentine ensign, now up and about, and suggested that the ensign and his crew move into smaller quarters in a ramshackle building adjoining ours. There was not enough of everything to go around, he insisted, and the paying tourists must come first. The young ensign rose to the occasion and made it quite plain that if anyone should freeze to death, it would be the courier himself and not the ship's crew. Emotions were running high.

*... chimney- like pinnacles ...*

Reluctant to use the communal pail, I left the shack to relieve myself during the height of the storm. Only by walking with the wind at my back and by cupping my hand over my nose could I breathe. All about me was a swirling gray world. Winds blowing through the cables that anchored the building to the ground produced a wild, howling whine. Back in the shack there was little to do but wrap up in a blanket and sit with my back to the wall.

How long, we were all wondering, would the storm last? Once it had blown itself out, would we be able to get back to the *Lapataia* without the landing craft? I found that when you are chilled to the bone, with no hope of changing the situation, nature seems to take over, and a delicious desire to sleep imbues you like a drug. Common sense tells you to get up and exercise, but the body rebels and longs only to sink into oblivion. My mind drifted to thoughts of Admundsen, Scott, Shackleton, Byrd, and Peary. How, in their right minds, could they have exchanged warmth and security for the tortures of cold, no matter how noble and gallant the quest?

After many hours of strange, abstract thoughts and fitful naps, I sensed that the building was becoming noticeably brighter. The winds seemed quieter.

During the night the *Lapataia* had moved from the bay to the leeward side of the narrow peninsula. When the winds dropped to about 30 knots, we walked outside and saw the *Lapataia* at her new anchorage, two miles away. Now, twenty-six hours after the storm began, we saw that two lifeboats, one with an inboard motor, were making toward shore. At a safe distance, seaward of the large incoming swells, the inboard motorboat dropped anchor, and the companion boat, attached by a line, headed straight toward the beach. Three crewmen in rubber wet suits kept the bow heading into the swells. We started loading. The elderly couple were quickly carried aboard. Then the man in the Brooks Brothers coat. The rest followed in orderly fashion. Pulling the line to the anchored motorboat, the crew took us off and after a quick transfer headed for the *Lapataia*.

The rescue operation took almost three hours. It was well handled, considering the dangerous heights of the swells pounding the shore. The two Argentine ladies saw to it that an inventory was taken of

... Chin-strap Penguins in the storm ...

what we had used and just before departure even swept the floors of the hut.

Devin and I were on the last trip. As we were leaving the bleak, rocky beach, several Gentoo Penguins stepped out from their snowbank storm shelters, shook themselves, and walked to the edge of the sea. Having weathered the storm in complete comfort, they seemed to be making sure we were departing, leaving them to their world, a world obviously alien to human intruders.

Back aboard we were restored by a hot shower (a special concession that day), dry clothing, coffee, and brandy.

Reflecting on our extraordinary experience and the general behavior of the group, I tried to assess my own responses. You always wonder how you will react in such a situation, the extent of courage or cowardice. One thing was certain. Despite the inevitable fears and discomforts, I had enjoyed the drama of it, being part of a unique adventure. In a sense it was for each of us an unexpected, head-on confrontation with the Antarctic.

Several months later, a commemorative bronze plaque was placed on a wall at Teniente Camara by the Argentine Government listing all our names and the names of the crew members and personnel who had withstood "un violento temporal."

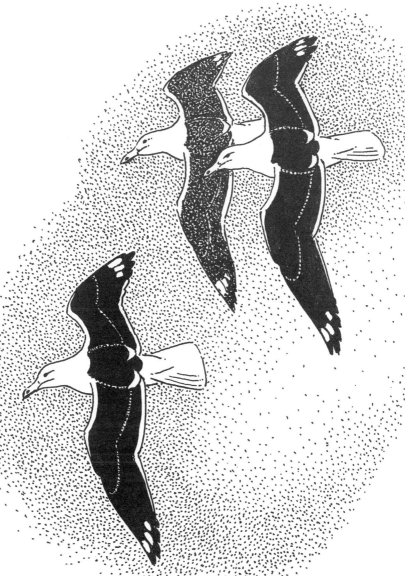

Kelp Gulls

BERING
SEA

YUKON R.

ALASKA

• EAGLE PASS

⊙ FAIRBANKS

CAMP DENALI → MT. McKINLEY
NATL. PARK
• PAXSON

MT. McKINLEY (DENALI)
20,320'

▷ — ST. PAUL
▷ — ST. GEORGE

PRIBILOF
ISLANDS

ANCHORAGE

ALASKA
PENINSULA

GULF OF ALASKA

COLD BAY
DUTCH HARBOR

UMNAK
ISLANDS

# Alaska - Mount McKinley Park

ALASKA POSSESSES an august grandeur that defies explanation. This breathtaking north country of 375 million acres, with its creatures, large and small, offers a gamut ranging from the world's largest carnivore, the brown bear, to the tiny hummingbird. Its wilderness is a home for vagrant species from Siberia and the Orient. Three to five new species are picked up annually by increasing numbers of alert birdwatchers.

Yet one of the greatest conservation battles has recently raged over its future. Should this last American wilderness remain unaltered, or is it to be ravaged? Who really should control Alaska and for what purpose? Who should decide its destiny?

Joined by Bob Clem and Ralph Palmer, I visited Alaska in June-July, 1968. Palmer and I had never met before, but I knew of his knowledge and fascination with the North Country. Upon receiving my invitation, he packed up his two young boys and drove from Albany, New York, to Charleston. He wanted to meet me and check me out. I must have passed his critical test, for we next met at O'Hare Airport prior to boarding a Northwest Orient flight to Anchorage. The American Ornithologists' Union was to convene at Fairbanks in mid-June, and we signed up for one of their preconvention field trips, scheduled to visit the Aleutian and Pribilof Islands.

Leaving Anchorage and its encircling snow mountains in a chartered Reeves Aleutian Airways DC-6, we flew along the north coast of the Alaskan peninsula, followed the island chain, landing at Cold

Bay and continuing on to spend a night on Umnak, where debris from World War II still littered the landscape.

As it turned out, our pilot was a birder, and, using the intercom, he gave us an airborne field trip, pointing out places of interest and the wildlife potential as we progressed westward. The plane brushed past volcanic mountain slopes, buzzed giant Brown Bears ambling over the tundra, and even flushed ptarmigan from the heather. We cruised the face of seabird cliffs at eye level, our pilot identifying various species from the hordes that occupied every ledge. Unfortunately, our closeness and the noise of the plane panicked many, causing them to pour off their perches in an avian avalanche, often knocking eggs into the sea. We won a race with a cruising Bald Eagle and joined thousands of feeding Slender-billed Shearwaters as we skimmed the surface of the Bering Sea.

Despite fog, the plane landed safely on St. Paul's Island, northernmost of the two larger Pribilof Islands. After we were assigned quarters in the small community, we walked down to the fur seal colonies along the rocky shoreline. Slipping over giant cablelike strands of glossy, olive-green kelp, we found ourselves among huge, one-ton fur seal bulls. They were spaced about a hundred feet apart, defending territories while awaiting the return of their harems. With long, drooping moustaches and rheumy eyes, many of the bellowing bulls sat conspicuously in the open. Others were harder to see as they blended in with the large beach boulders.

One of our group, Stuart Keith, unwittingly backed into an unseen bull while photographing. The animal made a quick, savage rush, bared its long, yellow, canine teeth, and tore an ugly gash in Keith's thigh. Fortunately, quick medical attention saved his leg.

The community of St. Paul's is perched on a hill. It consists of a cluster of buildings, some with gingerbread woodwork, and a church with an onion-shaped belfry, which reminded us that, not too long ago, these islands were owned by Russia. Warehouses stocked with metal drums and stacks of crates were also a sobering reminder that the harvest of seals was due to begin soon. Aleut Indians, who live on the mainland, come here in summer for the annual take.

Fifty thousand five-year-old males are killed each year for their fine, rich fur. There is a summer population of almost two million seals on the Pribilofs, so this cropping does not endanger the species.

One healthy bull may service a harem of from thirty to a hundred cows. With an even sex ratio of newborn pups, this leaves a sizable population of young bachelor bulls.

The culling operation is carefully supervised by the Fish and Wildlife Service, bringing in an annual six-million-dollar crop. Scarcely one skin has been miscounted over the past sixty years, and today the herd is increasing. Colin Bertram, of the Scott Polar Research Institution, calls the management of the fur seal herds "the finest example of the rational exploitation of any wild stock of animals."

The treeless, undulating interior of St. Paul's was thickly carpeted with lush grasses, wildflowers, nodding yellow poppies, and blue drifts of low lupine candles.

Small Arctic Foxes, skulking like alley cats, peered from behind rock outcroppings. Since it was June, they had exchanged their handsome white winter fur for mangy gray or black coats, and lurked close to the seabird cliffs, their source of food.

Standing on the summit of high, jagged cliffs, looking as far along the walls as the mist would allow, I saw that every ledge, cave, crevice, or hole was occupied by seabirds, tens of thousands of them.

... black and white upright murres ...

*Crested and Least Auklets...*

Delicate Kittiwake Gulls, Fulmars, upright black-and-white murres, both Horned and Tufted Puffins, Parakeet and Crested Auklets, and the tiny Least Auklet were perhaps the most numerous of all. The closest to us seemed nervous as they shuffled their varicolored webbed feet, deciding whether to hold their ground or take refuge in flight. Auks, auklets, murres, and puffins (all of them alcids) are the ecological northern counterpart of southern penguins, though not related. Far below, Red-faced and Pelagic Cormorants clustered together on the high ridges of wave-washed rocks. Some naturalists say that the Pribilof Islands hold the most concentrated population of birds on earth and that on a clear day a million alcids can be seen in the air at any given moment. This guessing game is made most difficult, as different species make their appearances at different times of the day.

En route to Fairbanks our birder pilot changed his course to show us several nesting Trumpeter Swans. These large white birds can be seen from miles away, usually sitting on muskrat island nests in small tundra ponds encircled by dark spruce forest.

Some time after midnight we were deposited on the campus of the University of Alaska, where we were given dormitory assignments. It was only two days from the shortest night in the year, and when I looked eastward, a cold blue sky sharply defined the outlines of giant spruce trees. A ceaseless chorus of Swainson's, Hermit, and Gray-cheeked Thrushes heralded the dawn, filling the short night with their glorious flutelike notes.

After the convention we rented a Hertz station wagon for the next three weeks, and, armed with detailed instructions for locating nesting Golden Eagles, Wandering Tattler, Wheatear, and ptarmigan, we left Fairbanks and headed a hundred miles northeast to a birding area called Eagle Pass. This was our initiation into the immense, forested mountain world of south-central Alaska. It was but a sampling of the relatively untouched splendors the forty-ninth state offers.

Wandering Tattler's nest . . . .

Following our instructions was like following clues on a treasure hunt. On one venture our first lead took us to an abandoned miner's shack off the main gravel road. It was a gem from the past, with its weathered boards, rusted stovepipe chimney, broken window, and bleached caribou horns nailed above the door.

Our next clue was a sentinel granite rock up the slope behind the shack. Still further up we found a stunted spruce with a white ribbon tied to one of the lower branches. There in the rain, perfectly camouflaged, brooding in a bower of flowering heather, mosses, and lichen, sat a Rock Ptarmigan. Crystal beads of water dotted her back. When I removed a twig above her head for a clearer camera shot, I touched her soft brown feathers. She spread both wings in a gesture intended to frighten the intruder. Instead of the usual white primaries, I saw each wing had been dyed, one red, the other blue. I then realized that this was a harmless scientific method for visual identification. But it was a shock to this unenlightened photographer.

miner's shack

*Mt. Denali*

Camp Denali is a privately owned and operated enterprise a few miles outside Mt. McKinley National Park. It became our base of operations. The camp's proprietor was Celia Hunter, a no-nonsense lady who is one of Alaska's most outspoken conservationists and a dedicated defender of the Alaskan wilderness.

Accommodations were simple but perfect for our needs. Our small half-tents (canvas above, wood below) were perched on a steep hillside and faced south, looking down a valley to distant forest, lakes, and glacial riverbeds. The view was unbelievably spectacular. In the background Mt. McKinley (the Indian name, Denali, meaning the Great One, is preferred) towered above a complex of lesser peaks, plateaus, and ridges. Standing white and alone, this tallest peak in North America is 20,320 feet of glistening ice fields and glaciers. After ten o'clock in the morning clouds and haze usually obscure it from sight, but once, at midnight, I saw the clouds part and reveal it bathed in deep salmon pink.

*Bohemian Waxwing . . .*
*silky and immaculate . . .*

A few feet from my tent a Bohemian Waxwing, silky and immaculate, sat patiently on her nest in a young spruce tree. Near at hand White-crowned Sparrows whistled and Varied Thrushes sang their haunting wheezy notes through the short subarctic night.

Our tents were equipped with sleeping bags, kerosene lantern, and a small wood stove. In the evening, when the breeze dropped, mosquitoes became unbearable.

After breakfast, with box lunches and camera gear, we took off in the station wagon. Generally Bob Clem and I would drop Ralph Palmer, a movie camera buff, at a beaver pond, moose bog, or a stream (outside the park), where he fished for grayling or kept watch on a nesting Water Ouzel. Very much the loner, Ralph possessed unlimited patience and enjoyed the sport of waiting for animals to come to him. The pictures he produced were excellent.

I was gratified by the ease with which we were able to approach moose, caribou, sheep, beaver, fox, marmot, and porcupine during our daily wanderings. Grizzly Bears were always at a distance, frosty-brown spots wandering over the tundra or half hidden in willow clumps. The wolves eluded us entirely.

I asked Ralph about the chances of photographing Dall Sheep. He answered: "If seen at all, they will be grazing high on the upper mountain slopes. Only a long climb might give you a chance at them."

The following morning, while driving the main park road near Polychrome Pass, we rounded a sharp curve. Bob jammed on the brakes as four Dall rams crossed ahead of us only a few feet in front of the car. Quite unafraid, they left the gravel road and walked down a steep incline to a nearby promontory ledge. There, in a bed of thick grass and wildflowers, they sat, displaying their spiraled horns with great elegance — "The silver ram with golden horns and jewel eyes" (Ernest Thompson Seton).

Dall Sheep ... quite unafraid

One afternoon I spotted a Red Fox vixen on her den mound, intently watching the valley below. With a camera in hand, I approached to within a few feet. She seemed unconcerned by my presence. Three small cubs came out of the den hole, their button-bright eyes never leaving me for a moment. The mother had not learned to fear man. Her attention was centered on a Golden Eagle circling the valley below us.

Most of McKinley Park, which embraces 3,000 square miles, is above timberline, providing uninterrupted vistas. Around us stretched green valleys, traced with moving cloud shadows, ornamented with bright-colored rocks, a spreading tapestry of wildflowers, mosses, and lichen, all strong, secure, vast, and free.

With knapsack over one shoulder, we often walked for hours over the tundra searching for nesting birds. Pink pillows of Moss Campion seemed to be everywhere. Blue-gray Reindeer Moss crunched under our feet.

Slopes that received little sunshine held patches of snow. Distant black specks in the snow, seen through binoculars, often proved to be groups of caribou. These animals are plagued by the tortures of Warble Flies, which enter their nostrils to lay eggs. They are the bane of the animals' summer existence. Apparently the cold of the snow and its reflected light give them some relief.

Vixen and cubs....

*Golden Plover*

The bubbling calls of curlew and the plaintive, fluted notes of Golden Plover often preceded the actual sighting of the callers. I am very familiar with the curlew's (Whimbrel) springtime music in the salt marshes at home, but here on the tundra it seemed to have a different dimension, epitomizing a solitary freedom.

Almost every lake had its nesting pair of loons, every glacial pond its scaup or Old-squaw Ducks, and every pothole its dainty red-necked Northern Phalaropes. Somewhere in each tundra valley a pair or two of Long-tailed Jaegers nested. Seen from afar the birds would hover, hawklike, over a certain spot, hoping to locate a mouse or lemming. If the nest and its chick could be located, the parent birds became absurdly tame. They would perch on one's head, pecking gently, a polite suggestion that the intruder leave. I managed to snap a fine close-up of Ralph Palmer wincing as a Long-tailed rested on his close-cropped head in the spread-eagle pose reminiscent of Prussian helmets.

Most shorebirds behaved well for the camera. Once a nest was located, the parent bird would depart, then within a few minutes return and quietly settle back on its eggs.

*... Caribou in snow bank ...*

Walter Spofford, an authority on birds of prey, had previously suggested making Paxson our headquarters. We could join him and his wife there and perhaps use his observation blinds. He was then doing a census study of Alaskan birds of prey. Paxson is a mere name on a map. It is about 160 miles east of the park and supports a combination inn and general store where two roads meet. Truckers, fishermen, and miners buy their supplies here, gas up their vehicles, eat, drop a coin or two in the jukebox, and swap stories. Nightly, bears raid the garbage dump behind the building.

Bordering the highway flowed a vodka-clear, rapid-moving stream, where scarlet Sockeye Salmon congregate by the thousands, their red, humped backs often breaking an inch above the water. Gravel bars in the stream's wider sections supported isolated pairs of nesting Arctic Terns, Spotted Sandpipers, and Lesser Yellowlegs. Robins, Song Sparrows, and Yellowthroats provided music from the willow thickets.

Spofford offered Bob and me the use of a blind he had constructed to overlook the aerie of a Golden Eagle. The small canvas contraption was perched on a narrow ledge near a mountaintop. It was like a brown limpet clinging to a giant boulder. Below it yawned a drop of several hundred feet to the valley below.

Eaglets, when very young, have to be fed often. The parent birds shuttle to and from the nest bringing meat that is then shredded into tidbits. As the fledglings grow, the parents return less often, and the size of the food morsels becomes larger. In later stages the parents return only once or twice a day, but they bring large items — squirrel, grouse, marmot, or rabbit.

We planned to enter the blind in the morning to take full advantage of sunlight. Armed with camera gear, sandwiches, and a few warm beers, we made the ten-mile drive from Paxson, then left the car near the mountaintop and worked our way afoot to the cliff ledge supporting the blind. Once inside we set up tripods, adjusted lenses for

... Long-Tailed Jaeger rested on his head...

distances, and focused on the nest not thirty feet away. The fledglings were about four weeks old now, with feathers showing through down. Undisturbed by our presence, the eaglets lay motionless in the pile of interwoven sticks, as if drugged by the warm sun.

We settled ourselves and adjusted to a hard seat on damp earth and cold stone and began our vigil. The sun was essential for good photography. We figured that it would be gone from the cliff face by three o'clock in the afternoon, leaving the nest in shadow. After six hours of waiting, the sun began to creep away from the face of the cliff. Neither of the parent birds had made an appearance.

Disappointed, huddling in our uncomfortable cocoon, we watched the inevitable dark-blue swathe of shadow reach across the stone. It was just about to touch the nest itself when the two eaglets suddenly awoke, stood on wobbly, trousered legs, and looked about. A shadow flashed by, and with a whooshing sound a parent bird alit and folded her great wings. She posed briefly on the ledge of the nest, just long enough to drop half a marmot for the young, glanced over one tawny shoulder, then launched into a long glide and vanished down into the valley below. Having both cameras prefocused, we found that the ten-second visit allowed each of us time to click off four frames before the bird was gone.

Suddenly it was a wonderful day, well worth the discomforts and endless waiting. The photographic results were more than respectable.

How long can Alaska hold back the modern onrushing exploiters? Only the setting aside of vast areas of wilderness, backed by the strictest laws, can save this magnificent land.

Golden Eagle .... posed briefly

What would the world be, once bereft
Of wet and of wilderness? Let them be left,
O let them be left, wildness and wet;
Long live the weeds and the wilderness yet.
— Gerard Manley Hopkins
(1844-89)

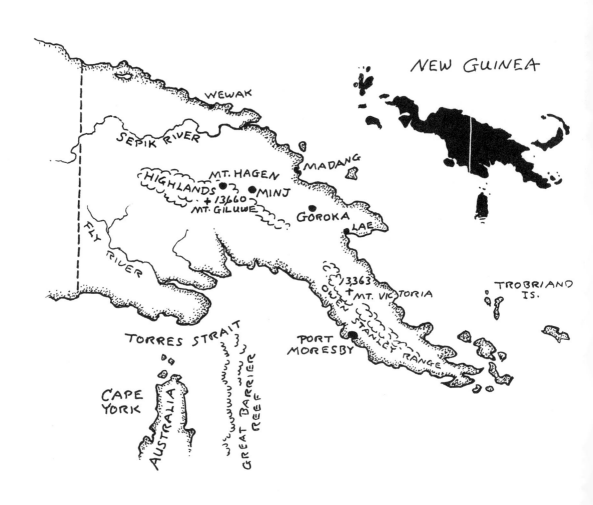

NEW GUINEA

WEWAK

SEPIK RIVER

MADANG

MT. HAGEN

HIGHLANDS

MINJ

+ 13660
MT. GILUWE

GOROKA

LAE

FLY RIVER

13363
+ MT. VICTORIA

OWEN STANLEY RANGE

TROBRIAND IS.

TORRES STRAIT

PORT MORESBY

CAPE YORK

AUSTRALIA

GREAT BARRIER REEF

# New Guinea - The Stone Age and Birds of Paradise

IN 1957, WHILE ATTENDING an Audubon Society Convention in Boston, I met E. Thomas Gilliard, then an associate curator of birds at the New York American Museum of Natural History, where he remained until his untimely death in 1965. He had just returned from his fifth expedition to New Guinea to study, collect, and photograph its birds. For a good two hours he kept me enthralled with his tales and contagious enthusiasm for New Guinea. I asked him about the status of that most beautiful, bizarre, and exotic of all birds, the Bird of Paradise. Were they still plentiful or had they suffered irretrievably from the feather trade? He led me to believe that most species were still in good shape, despite the great pressures of the trade, and he painted a word picture of a group of courting males that I have never forgotten.

Fifteen years later, my name now familiar to the Lindblad Travel Agency, I began to receive tempting folders on New Guinea. In addition to tours about the Papuan highland towns, the itinerary offered a week's cruise on the Sepik River. My much-traveled friend, Gertrude Legendre, and I both signed up. New Guinea was one of the few primitive places in the world she had never visited — nor had I.

We left California on October 11, with stops en route at Honolulu and the Fiji Islands. Around breakfast time the tan-colored cliffs of New South Wales came into view. A half-hour later the big jet took a long swing above the red-tiled rooftops of suburban Sydney and made an easy landing.

Once established at the Hotel Wentworth, still somewhat bewildered and excited at finding myself on a new continent, I took my binoculars and headed for the botanical gardens two blocks away. Sydney, with its new glass skyscrapers, sparkled after the night's rain. Ultramodern fountains of different shapes and patterns threw their spume onto the streets and sidewalks. The sprawling harbor was dotted with white sails as various regattas fought a brisk wind. From the hillside gardens I could see the huge, curved, shell-like arches of the controversial new opera house protruding into the bay. Strolling about the park, I identified a few common Australian birds, and was thrilled to see several tiny turquoise-and-black Variegated Fairy Wrens, one of Australia's most colorful avian families. New

Variegated Fairy Wren

New Guinea
... a land of mountains and clouds

birds and jet lag suddenly overtook me, and in a zombielike trance I wandered back to the hotel for the longest sleep I can remember.

On our third morning in Sydney, following instructions, we piled our luggage in the lobby, taxied to the airport, and, boarding an Ansett jet, flew north over eastern Australia, then out to sea over parts of the Great Barrier Reef with its countless shoals of brilliant blues and greens and pale crescent sands.

After a five-hour flight we disembarked at Port Moresby in a blast of dry heat. The surrounding hills, smoking with brush fires, were burnt brown. Numerous dust devils swirled about. There was a long wait in a hangar before we boarded a two-prop De Havilland Otter, one of the great workhorse planes of World War II. Our group and its gear occupied every seat; we were packed like fish in a tin. The plane took off, left the brown lowland hills behind, and climbed up over the lush green mountains of central-eastern New Guinea.

New Guinea! The name has always had an exciting ring to it. So few westerners have ever been there. This, the world's second largest island (after Greenland), is shaped not unlike a legless lizard with a great open jaw snapping in a northwesterly direction at the Indonesian islands. It is 1,500 miles long, the narrower parts of the neck and tail being one or two hundred miles wide, and the enlarged belly perhaps 500 miles wide. Topographically it is composed of numerous high mountain ranges in dramatic spines that run the length of the lizard. Several of the highest ranges are snow-capped, with Mt. Carstens Toppen the highest at 16,500 feet.

Although roads are scarce, there are a few in the Papuan highlands and others that connect some coastal towns. The great bulk of New Guinea is still totally primitive. To quote from Gilliard's book, *Birds of Paradise and Bower Birds*, published in 1969:

> A few years back I flew 1,000 miles along the northern coast of New Guinea a few days after flying across the deforested overpopulated subcontinent of Southeast Asia. The contrast of what I saw was staggering. I found myself gazing, hour after hour, in admiration and disbelief of New Guinea's "endless forests." Only rarely could I see a trace of the workings of man. One has to see it to believe it. By way of an analogy I should say that if a football field represented the forests of New Guinea as they stood on the day that man first arrived, then a postage stamp cut into slivers and scattered over the field would represent the total amount of forest that man has altered or obliterated since his arrival.

The endless mountain ranges are geologically "young"; hence their extraordinary rugged and sharp-edged appearance. Native trails were easily visible from the air. They followed the ridge edges — and for good reason. The steep slopes made them inaccessible, and ridges provided good visibility for spotting an enemy. With an average rainfall of from 55 to 300 inches a year, the forested floors at such steep angles shed their excess waters into rushing streams that more often than not were in a state of torrential chaos.

Mountain ranges that run 1,000 miles down the length of New Guinea form such steep barrier walls that many biologically isolated pockets have been created. Plants, birds, mammals, and in some cases even men have formed quite different subspecies, though they live only a few miles apart. Several species of Birds of Paradise are striking instances of this evolutionary phenomenon. A Bird of Paradise whose flank plumes are blood red might live on the south side of a mountain, but less than a mile distant, across a pass, the same species has yellow-orange plumes.

The two million people of New Guinea have been isolated by these same physical barriers of mountain walls and torrential streams. In fact, this isolation has created more than seven hundred dialects! Native skin color ranges from black-black to light brown; height varies from six-footers to four-foot pygmies; lips from thin to thick; and hair from kinky to straight. Most natives have never seen a white man, and few have ever seen a wheel. The last great population of Stone Age men lives in New Guinea.

Born as trickles from melting snows and rain, many large rivers tumble down the north and south slopes to the flat alluvial plains,

where they then flow slowly hundreds of miles to the sea. On the flats the rivers wind in oxbows and loops that create many crescent-shaped lakes. These jungle rivers have just about everything a romantic ever dreamed of — crocodiles, bands of nomadic headhunters, beautifully carved and painted war canoes, droves of water birds, colorful parrots, and lotus blossoms on stems six feet tall.

Our short flights over the Papuan highlands were seldom pleasant ones. The Otter aircraft was broad-winged and slow. Sometimes we took off in brilliant sunshine and within minutes were flying into black thunderheads and violent rain squalls. Sudden winds would buffet the plane from all directions. We often had to circle a mountain airstrip many times, waiting for an opening in the clouds for a safe landing.

Seated one afternoon in the copilot's seat, I was marveling at this world of mountains and clouds. The pilot turned to me and made a timely remark: "One thing I have learned flying here is that if you see a cloud in New Guinea, you can bet your last dollar that somewhere in it there's a mountain."

The small towns we stayed in were Kundiawa, Goroka, Minj, and Mount Hagen. Founded by European or Australian farming settlers, all had comfortable lodges with hot water, good food, and excellent Dutch beer.

At Minj, an agricultural community walled in by mountains, there was a European population of about 150. Their good life included a nine-hole golf course and two perfectly kept grass tennis courts. The small, freshly painted Anglican church was holding Sunday services as I walked by the open door. The organ boomed as the minister conducted a communion service for five persons.

Highland birding was rather frustrating. Most birds I could not identify. I had little previous knowledge of New Guinea birds, and there was no field guide available. I did recognize wagtails, crows, and one or two honey-eaters. In town large eucalyptus trees were often filled with small, pointed-tailed, screeching lorrikeets. Like a flurry of green leaves they would generally vanish just as I trained my binoculars on them.

Early one morning at Minj I was walking the dew-drenched golf course and peered down into a heavily forested ravine just off the

*Victoria Crested Pigeon*

fairway. Suddenly a rather nondescript, robin-sized bird, uttering loud metallic calls, flew down the valley and disappeared. The dark, wine-colored body and pale yellowish head were enough to identify it as a Bird of Paradise, the creature I had flown half way around the world to see. This one was an immature, plumeless male of either the Lesser or Raggiana variety.

Two Volkswagen buses drove us about the highlands. We stopped at spectacular viewing points, crawled into caves, walked about the countryside, watched "sing-sing" dances, and visited village market places.

Beside a dirt road New Guineans would gather to socialize and sell their excess produce of fruit, vegetables, and tubers, many piled on rush mats. There were also new baskets for sale, as well as pigs and chickens tied together by their legs. Most men wore well-used and patched khaki shorts, and torn T-shirts. Mothers sat by their produce and nursed their infants, as well as children aged two or three. Scattered about were a few male dandies and village belles, all in full tribal regalia, returning from a sing-sing. They sported paradise plumes, parrot feathers, crowned pigeon crests, owl wings, eagle feathers, hibiscus, croton and fern leaves, many items woven into tight wool caps. An occasional Bird of Paradise skin was offered for sale. Held up like a lollipop on a stick, its asking price was about ten dollars. Examining them carefully, I understood their fascination. No man-made fabric or material could possibly compete with the plumes' ethereal gossamer texture. I would have given a good deal to

The Mud Men

own one or two of the skins. There is no law to prevent their sale, but the law is strict in prohibiting their being taken out of the country. I abandoned hope when I realized that I did not have the makings of a successful smuggler.

Sing-sings, or tribal dances, are very important to the New Guinea native. They are a form of self-expression, used to commemorate battles won, deaths, births, and the history of the clan. They also give the individual a chance to display himself, his wealth in ornaments, shells, furs, and, especially, bird plumes. The spontaneous sing-sings we happened upon were apparently a rather common occurrence and spectacular. In contrast, the prearranged ceremonies for the new breed of tourist were half-hearted, dismal affairs.

An example of the latter was the much-publicized performance of the mud men from a tribal village outside Goroka. For cash they reenacted a victorious battle of long ago when a small tribe completely vanquished a numerically superior neighboring enemy. Covering themselves with gray clay and wearing oversized, grotesque clay masks, the mud men rushed the enemy, who, at sight of them, turned on their heels and beat a hasty retreat.

Several years ago the Canadian Club whisky firm sent their cameramen to photograph the mud men in mock attack, and the ad depicting them found its way into many English-speaking magazines around the world. We watched and photographed the mud men's act, and I could imagine the chief shouting orders as our Volkswagen caravan rounded the curve: "Drop the cigarettes, hide the Coke bottles, slap on the mud, and look fierce. Here we go again!"

In complete contrast we happened one day upon a tribal sing-sing near Mt. Hagen, off the road in a coconut palm grove. Sixty men, dressed in similar regalia, stood in ranks five abreast, with all their personal wealth on display in the form of spectacular feathers. Beating long, spoon-shaped drums, muscular bodies shining with sweat, they jogged and jumped together in perfect unison. All wore a Tree Wallaby skin about the neck, circular loops of enamel-blue King of Saxony Bird of Paradise head plumes, undoubtedly the most bizarre feathers from any bird on earth, through their nostrils. Fresh green leaves looped over their belt in the rear gave the effect of a rooster's tail.

The actual headdress was a marvel. Apricot-colored paradise plumes billowed out from a bristling base of scarlet parrot feathers, and topping this towered eight or ten very long, velvety-black tail feathers from the Princess Stephanie Bird of Paradise. The plumes trembled and waved with the contagious rhythms of drums and chanting voices. Until we arrived on the scene, the whole elaborate show was being watched by only a handful of tribal members.

We happened on many other sing-sings in our short visit, but none had the style and sheer beauty of the first one. Some involved more participants, including women and children. One rather fierce all-male group asked us to leave. We awkwardly lingered awhile watching the dance, awed by the huge headdresses of brown barred eagle feathers and evil-looking barbed spears. The natives resented our presence, and in the heat of the dance the chief broke ranks, singled me out because of my height, and hurled a spear over my shoulder as I was photographing him. I don't believe his intentions were serious, but it was an unmistakable gesture, and we left.

Signs of changing times were seen in many of the tribal getups. One man I noticed sported two red plastic golf tees driven into his nostrils. Bits of bright aluminum foil and colored labels from tin cans were evident, as well as other gaudy bits and pieces from the white man's trash piles. Most amazing of all, some paradise plumes were now dyed bright pink or purple.

Perhaps the beginning of this disintegration of tribal taste, inventiveness, and pride can be traced to the annual sing-sing gathering at Mt. Hagen. This is the largest and most dazzling show in the entire South Pacific. It has been slowly built up as an attraction for tourists and participants alike. As many as 75,000 highland natives gather in competition for two days in the open fields and bring with them their precious plumes. They come for miles (often a walk of over three days) with their headdresses carefully wrapped in palm fronds, banana leaves, or old newspapers. From dawn to dusk the drums boom, the earth shakes with pounding feet, and the entire village of Mt. Hagen shimmers under a blanket of Bird of Paradise plumes.

This gathering creates a mutual tolerance among tribes who only yesterday were deadly enemies. They now compare outfits and borrow ideas from each other in song and dance. But their unique individuality, preserved by tribal pride and protected by isolation, is rapidly vanishing.

*... the headdress was a marvel ...*

One day, while driving through mountain country, we stopped at a vantage lookout point. Walking away, I happened to see a lone native, standing on a rock, watching roadwork being done fifty feet below him. He was a dignified, naked figure with headdress ablaze with plumes. Three enormous yellow caterpillar earth-movers were grinding away at the mountainside, building a highway. Japanese engineers in black business suits were discussing problems with an Italian construction foreman. The solitary native had the expression of a bewildered child. Something was happening to his homeland, something he was unable to comprehend.

Birds of Paradise have played a large role in the history and economy of New Guinea. The true Birds of Paradise number about forty-three species.

In the early days of the Christian era gorgeous feathers of Birds of Paradise began to drift westward via Asia to eastern Europe, but it was not until 1600 that the skins appeared regularly on the European market. These were elongated skins wrapped about a stick and legless, hence the term "paradise," which had a twofold meaning: Not only were they beautiful, but, being legless, the birds must be completely ethereal, never landing but forever flying somewhere between earth and heaven.

The first naturalist to report seeing a Bird of Paradise in the wilds was a Frenchman, René P. Lesson. On a voyage of discovery aboard the corvette *La Coquille,* he landed in New Guinea in 1824 and collected four species, among which were the little King and the Lesser Bird of Paradise.

The next great naturalist to study the birds alive was Alfred Russel Wallace, contemporary and good friend of Charles Darwin and co-originator of the theory of evolution. From then on, the discoveries of naturalists are well documented. Unfortunately, the plume hunters, who began to flood the capitals of Europe with bird skins by the thousands, attached no tags or markings to indicate where they had been collected.

Germany, during her brief colonizing effort in the South Pacific, established a claim to the northern half of New Guinea. Copra plantations were developed, but during the seven-year wait for the first crop to mature, Paradise skins were collected for export, and they became the chief source of revenue.

*King of Saxony Bird of Paradise*
*... the most bizarre feathers on earth ...*

During this period many of the birds were named after German royalty and became a veritable social register of crowned heads — Emperor of Germany, King of Saxony, Prince Rudolf, Augusta Victoria, and Princess Stephanie, to mention a few.

There seems to be no question that the chief export of New Guinea from 1890 to 1910 was plumes. Staggering figures reveal that around 10,000 skins were exported from German New Guinea annually until the onset of World War I. In 1912 a British firm received, in one shipment, 28,000 skins, and it is estimated that during this period at least 80,000 skins were shipped from New Guinea and adjacent islands.

The economic importance of the trade was obvious, but about that same time there developed a worldwide revulsion against such mass slaughter. Several species of birds, especially in America, had just

*... a male in ecstatic pose ...*

become extinct (Carolina Parakeet, Labrador Duck, and the Passenger Pigeon, whose numbers in the past century were estimated in the billions). The Audubon Society was created about this time, and the extermination of birds for their plumes in America ceased. Notable was the ban on egret feathers for women's hats. By 1913 the importation of all bird plumage in the United States was prohibited by the Wilson Tariff Act. Shortly thereafter, Holland, Canada, England, and Australia followed suit.

Gilliard firmly believed that this conservation breakthrough, coupled with New Guinea's impenetrable, rugged terrain and virgin wilderness, would keep these birds in healthy numbers for years to come. Another point in their favor is the fact that only adult males in full plumage are collected. The females and young males capable of breeding before the plumes appear insure the birds' continued existence.

Sir Edward Hallstrom, a burly Australian philanthropist and frequent visitor to New Guinea (he died in 1971), was completely absorbed with Birds of Paradise. He firmly believed that they were headed toward extinction, and developed the Baiyer River Sanctuary for their study and protection. Well-built aviaries with gravel walkways and mowed lawns were situated in the center of a river-bordered forest. Its collection of New Guinea birds was then undoubtedly the finest in the world. There were at least twelve species of *paradisaea*, as well as Green Catbirds, Manucodes, Crowned Pigeons, Hornbills, and Cassowaries. The Paradise aviaries were now fenced with heavy half-inch wire to keep out snakes, which had been a serious problem.

Several of the male *paradisaea* were strangely stimulated by the close proximity of people. A male Reggiana, as I approached his cage, hopped to the nearest branch all atremble as his scarlet-and-orange plumes billowed out into a large powder puff. The little King, a velvety crimson gem of a bird, clung to the wire only inches from me, and showed off his white-and-green false side wings and his tightly curled green pennants attached to the ends of two curved, wirelike tailshafts.

Walking about the neighboring forest, I saw Lesser Birds of Paradise all about us, enjoying the protection of the sanctuary, or perhaps attracted by the sounds of their captive relatives. Their loud, gonglike calls rang through the sun-dappled forest. Although I saw at least fifty or sixty wild birds, only three were adult males, and only one of these displayed. High over my head, hopping about a bare branch, this male in ecstatic pose touched the branch with his bill, bowed his wings and fluttered his opened plumes, spotlit in the warm afternoon rays of the sun. This display excited females and immature males, who also hopped about and flew in and out of the area. My thoughts again returned to Tom Gilliard and his description of such happenings fifteen years before, when we met in Boston.

Boarding another Otter, we left the highlands and headed north-westward until clouds and mountains faded behind us. Flying low, we were in a new world of marshy wetlands that stretched to the horizon. A great tannish-green river appeared, twisting like a giant snake. This was the Sepik, New Guinea's second longest river, which is navigable for about 550 of its 700 miles. Our final flight destination came into view.

At a simple grass airstrip near the village of Ambunti the plane landed and we disembarked. Awaiting us was Wayne Heathcote, owner and captain of the houseboat on which we would travel. We found him to be a most agreeable young Australian with a superb accent. He had been a patrol officer on the river for four years, then became a dealer in crocodile hides and collector of primitive Sepik River art. The tribal chiefs were all his friends.

The houseboat was tied up to a crude landing. Our new floating home was a 70-foot-long box on pontoons propelled by two

*···our···70-foot-long floating home···*

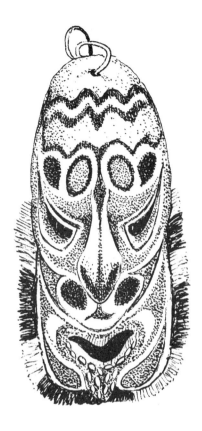

*Sepik River mask*

110-horsepower outboard motors. Once on board we found everything surprisingly neat and orderly. At the bow was the social room where we sat and ate. Amidships were ten double-decker cabins. Each had an electric wall fan, numerous hooks for clothing, and a large screened window. There were three "heads" and showers. Astern was the galley and storage rooms. The eight-man native crew slept anywhere they could. Behind the wheelhouse, on the upper deck, was an open area with deck chairs and a railing generally ablaze with drying laundry. All in all, it worked well. The bar was well stocked. The food was excellent and often featured curries and lots of fresh fruit.

Daily life aboard was simple, unhurried, and altogether fascinating. The great muddy river rolled on at an even pace of about three knots. There were few navigational hazards except for floating logs and islands of "pit-pit" grass that had broken away from the shore and were being carried seaward with the current. Men in dugout canoes with spearlike paddles flashing wet in the sun plied the river both ways. At night we tied up to a crude village levee, or simply threw a rope around a stout tree. Tropical downpours were frequent but never lasted long.

While cruising the Sepik I spent much time on the top deck looking for birds and crocodiles. I soon discovered that floating logs and crocodiles looked alike. Behind the tall, bordering "pit-pit" grass, forests of giant trees, weeping with flowering vines, lianas, and

.... on the Sepik River ....

climbing palms, slowly slipped by. From their dark recesses I could hear the clanging calls of Birds of Paradise, distinctive from the calls of other forest birds. Flocks of Sulphur-crested Cockatoos were visible from a mile away when they gathered on the exposed branches of dead trees. Occasionally brilliant Eclectus Parrots in pairs flew overhead with the stiff-shouldered flight of most parrots; the male is all green with red wings, the female is very different, red with blue wings. Several White-bellied Sea Eagles and Brahminy Kites were seen, and Black Kites often circled the boat scavenging for garbage.

Daily we took excursions from the mother boat in two outboard launches. Endless tributaries and natural canals were explored. Some reached a dead end, while others wound their way through corridors of grass and eventually into a lake, some with stands of giant pink lotus. Mudskippers, small amphibian fish with popeyes, hopped over mud and logs when disturbed by our wake. Unexplained were backwater areas where giant catfish had died by the thousands, bloated and floating on their sides.

Wherever the launch went we disturbed hordes of roosting cormorants, darters, and various species of herons. In open water Spotted Whistling Ducks and Australian Black Ducks gathered in large rafts. Tiny, teal-size Green Pygmy Geese swam through beds of water lilies, barely visible amongst the floating plants. At the slightest breeze leaf pads, green on top and purple beneath, would flip over like pages in a book. Here too were large Purple Swamp Hens and long-toed Lotus Birds (Jacanas) with flesh-pink facial wattles walking over the vegetation.

By chance one morning we passed under a large tree whose branches seemed to be laden with furry seedpods. Suddenly the tree exploded and hundreds of fruit bats, or "flying foxes," took to the air squealing, and flapped about slowly on four-foot wings. After the boat was well away, they returned to their upside-down sleeping position and became "seedpods" once more. Several times the two launches landed at a village hidden in some tributary miles from the main body of the Sepik. Many of the inhabitants had never seen tourists before. Their only exposure to white men had been the occasional patrol officers checking on the now outlawed practice of cannibalism or hunting for artifacts.

Wandering about these villages, I was struck by the earthy simplicity and the undisturbed attitude of the people. Here the aborigines were coffee-colored, short, well-built people with kinky hair and wide flat nostrils. Thin-limbed, swollen-bellied children, with sullen underfed dogs, followed us at a distance. All the thatch-and-pole houses were built high up on stilts, ten feet or more above ground, to avoid the extremes of seasonal river flooding. The fronts of many houses had bark and wood carvings, often brightly painted with

*Pied Heron on dugout bow*

natural dyes and resembling grotesque human masks, the purpose of which was to ward away the evil river spirits. A notched log ladder led to the elevated flooring of bark and bamboo, where old people sat weaving, gossiping, and smoking. Their expectorations of betelnut juice had formed a red ring on the ground around each house.

Overhead, giving shade from the searing sun, towered coconut palms, slender betelnut palms, mango, and breadfruit. Harsh cries of Friarbirds rang out to disturb the noonday quiet. On the hard smooth ground, packed by the footsteps of years, pigs, chickens, and Muscovy Ducks wandered. Occasionally a beautifully marked Cassowary

*Terminal ridge poles resembled... gargoyles...*

chick that had been caught in the wilds scratched about with the chickens.

A few children carried a pet cuscus around their necks. The unhappy creatures, nocturnal tree possums, tortured by the bright sunlight, blinked their runny eyes. I was led to believe that pets and dogs eventually all ended in the cooking pot. Village women who wove mats and baskets, pounded the pulp of Sago palms into the floury paste that was their mainstay. This dough they shaped by hand into flat cakes, which they then fried over a fire, even as they nursed children, smoked, and gossiped. Men carved wooden masks, hollowed out their great canoes, set out fishnets and traps in the river, or went hunting for crocodiles. In their brown nakedness they wore only odd bits and pieces of clothing, sometimes little more than a penis sheath. They ogled our varied attire of hats and strange clothing, which we suddenly felt to be not only uncomfortable, but badly out of place.

Most villages have a cult house, or *tamboran*, which is a combination male clubhouse (where rituals are performed), a repository of cultural artifacts, and a place to house the skulls of chiefs , warriors, and enemies alike. Most important of all, it is a shelter that preserves tribal identity. Some of these structures are beautiful in both design and decoration. Large tamborans could be 100 feet long, and the ridge pole supporting the thatch roof 60 feet above the ground. Roof ends sweep upward and may resemble the gape of a giant crocodile. Terminal ridge pole ends are generally intricately carved as weird gargoyles. The most common design was a large cormorantlike bird in a mating embrace with a crocodile. The ceiling was made of sheets of pounded bark ornately painted in natural dyes to depict skulls, masks, birds, plants, reptiles, all interwoven in intricate designs. They brought to mind the paintings of Picasso; the similarity was startling. I wondered if this artist and the post-Impressionist school had been influenced by the South Pacific artisans, and if so, when and how?

The afternoon of our last day on the river we visited the great tamboran house at the village of Kanganaman. This was the tallest and largest tamboran on the Sepik, protected by a forest of towering palms through which the afternoon light filtered and ornamented the leaf-strewn ground with irregular golden patches.

Once inside the dark cult house, when our eyes became accustomed to the gloom, we noticed men sitting about on the hard-packed earth or on raised planks, talking and smoking, guarding their artifacts. Most of the dusty objects were for sale. Walking about in the half-light, I barely made out in the dusky corner the outline of a carved reptile-bird ridge pole gargoyle. Lifting the five-foot object by its serpentine neck, I carried it outside into the light and gazed at its graceful contours and superb carving. Its owner rushed after me saying "hundred dollar." I replied, "Eighty." He said "O.K." The whole transaction was hard to believe. I was very pleased with myself. I realized I had discovered the best buy by far; it had museum quality.

Nightly after supper Wayne Heathcote would sit on a step of the companionway of our houseboat and say in his finest Australian accent: "Good evening, ladies and gentlemen. I hope you've 'ad a good day. I'll run through what we've already seen and tell you about tomorrow's plans." Numerous questions and answers followed, and the ever-popular subject of cannibalism would crop up. Yes, it was still practiced. He mentioned that village life beyond that second range of blue mountains, away from the eyes of police patrols, hadn't changed much. With a diet heavy in starches, meat is essential for survival. No protein could be wasted. Beyond the food value there was also a strong belief that the finest qualities of the late-departed could be acquired by consumption.

Among many stories of tribal behavior, happenings on the river, some shocking, some humorous, some even pathetic, one tale I recall vividly. It was handed down from the days of World War II. It concerns an American Army base near the coast during the last phase of the Pacific war. At the height of activities a particular tribal chieftain often walked down from his hilltop village to watch the goings-on at the base. He would marvel at the bustle of vehicles and people. Dressed in his finest cod-piece, cowrie shell necklaces and feathered headdress, he soon became a fixture at the establishment, just watching and never bothering anyone. To him the enlisted men's club was the most fascinating place of all. Here were the colorful jukeboxes, Coke and pinball machines, radios, and all types of wondrous, noisy, flashing things.

The war ended and everyone departed, leaving the broken magic toys to sit there and rust. With his strongest warriors in tow, the chief hauled out as many of the heavy bulky machines as he could; he strapped them to poles and had them carried through miles of jungle, across torrential streams, and up the steep hillsides to his village.

Once there he gathered the tribe about the strange, colorful objects, and waited for something to happen. But no lights flashed, no wondrous sounds came from the gorgeous machines that once had moving rainbows and ascending white bubbles; no cold, bottled cola popped from the red box. Nothing happened at all. Only the bark of a dog, the wail of an infant, the screech of parrots, and the familiar sound of rain dripping from the wet leaves were heard. The chief gathered his council together, and they decided that the once friendly

but odd brothers from distant lands had betrayed them. There was only one thing left to do, declare war on the United States of America.

I enjoy my Sepik objets d'art, but, more vividly, I enjoy memories of the great river — that chance to savor its grandeur, its colorful wildlife, and its mysterious and primitive culture before it changes and much of it is lost.

Bachman's Warbler

# Birding in India

ONE DAY IN APRIL, 1960, while I was painting in my studio the phone rang. Several quarters clanked into the machine before a voice spoke. "John Dick, this is Ben King. I'm in the Navy, stationed at San Diego. I am a serious birder, and I hear, through friends, that a Bachman's Warbler has been seen in your area."

"Yes," I said. "I saw it last week, a male, singing on territory."

"If I can catch a navy plane to Charleston tonight, could you pick me up and take me to the location?"

"Yes, but I can't guarantee the bird. We'll try. I'll pick you up at 7:30 tomorrow morning."

He was there at the designated meeting place on schedule, a young man in his twenties with dark curly hair. He wore a sailor's uniform, pea jacket, and carried a small black bag. Without much talk we drove the thirty miles to the Moore's Landing road south of McClellanville. About one mile before the landing, in thick pine woods, we stopped and walked about, hunting for America's rarest songbird, a bird that few of the ornithological giants had ever seen.

Within ten minutes, amid the songs of a Summer Tanager, Cardinal, Pine, Parula, and Yellow-throated Warblers, and a Yellow-breasted Chat or two, King called out, "I have it!" His keen eye had spotted this much sought-after rarity. We watched the male halfway up a loblolly pine at the end of a dead branch. The tiny bird threw his head back, exposing his trademark, the black bib and yellow belly. With wings and tail aquiver, he produced a short song, something between the trills of a Parula Warbler and a Chipping Sparrow.

King pulled out a small black notebook and wrote a few sentences. I then returned him to the Navy side of the airport, where he caught a flight back to San Diego. Within twenty-four hours he had flown six thousand miles and seen one of the world's rarest and least-known birds. The whole trip had cost him no more than the price of a phone call. I did not hear from Ben King again for eleven years.

In March, 1971, he phoned me. "John, this is Ben King. Since I last saw you I have been living and traveling through the Orient—Japan, Korea, Hong Kong. But mostly I've been working in Thailand, living on various grants, writing and collecting for various museums. I have just completed the text for a forthcoming book, *A Field Guide to the Birds of Southeast Asia*. Now I'm starting a new project, and am writing the text for *A Guide to the Birds of India*. Would you be interested in doing the illustrations for it? It will involve about 1,300 species with their different plumages according to sex, age, and variations."

After a week of weighing the pros and cons, I returned his call and gave him an affirmative "Yes." When final decisions were made as to size of the paintings and general format, I started working. Each original was to be 19 by 27 inches and painted on Crescent light-gray illustration board. I decided to start with the birds I knew best, the ducks. These were followed by geese, cranes, storks, and ibis. Then I would tackle the glamorous pheasants, partridge, herons, and so on. I became totally absorbed.

Skins of all Indian birds (except for the larger eagles and water fowl) were shipped to me in crates from the bird department of the American Museum of Natural History in New York. These skins had been carefully picked out by King. The museum has a wise policy of not releasing a skin if there are less than five specimens in their collection. These rarities were carefully photographed by King at close range, from front, side, and back, and the slides sent to me.

In October, 1972, therefore, after our three weeks' adventure in New Guinea, Gertie and I parted company in Sydney, Australia. I flew east to India's New Delhi.

Ben King then was living there under a Fulbright Foundation grant and was collecting material and expanding his knowledge of Indian birds. He had organized a two-week concentrated birding trip for me. It was essential that I become more familiar with new species and, especially, the bird families of the great subcontinent.

I left Australia on November 6 and flew to Hong Kong, arriving in the early evening, the plane passing low over the burnt-out hull of the *Queen Elizabeth* lying on her side in the bay. Airborne again, flying inland, I looked down on the darkened Asian landscape, lit not by the blazing star patterns of the cities of the Western World but by weak traceries of lights, as delicate as spider webs.

Because the legal entanglements of renting one's own car are legion, we settled for hiring a driver with his own antique taxi, an Ambassador, manufactured in India.

We headed north. Only someone born in India has the gall to plunge into the mainstream of city traffic. It reminded me of a two-way endless stream of army ants moving across the floor of a rain

Temple in Red Fort ... Delhi

forest. One must plow through masses of humanity, hoping to avoid Brahmin priests in rickshaws, wandering sacred cattle, bicycles, groaning bullock carts, brightly painted, overloaded buses, stray dogs, strings of camels carrying charcoal, and holy men sitting cross-legged in the road.

Amid this confusion birds were everywhere. At likely spots such as brushy weed patches, wooded edges of the road, and marshy borders we stopped to stretch our legs. In this world birds and man have coexisted for so many centuries that they hardly seem to notice each other. Vultures, storks, plovers, crows, drongos, bulbuls, parakeets, doves, mynas, shrikes, and herons all are woven into that vast tapestry called India.

Our destination was 250 miles north of New Delhi, the old British resort hill station of Mussorie. This town is saddled on the crest of a hill with a view to the south, overlooking the great sweltering plain and the sluggish, meandering Ganges River. Far away to the north is the silent Himalayan massif.

We arrived at Mussorie in the early evening. Struggling up a very steep incline toward the hotel, the clutch of our Ambassador broke. So we made the last few hundred feet on foot, carrying our luggage. Our hotel, the Savoy, was almost unoccupied.

Our quarters on the second floor overlooked a courtyard. They were sparsely furnished and consisted of a living room, bedrooms, and bath. In many such old hotels in India lighting fixtures are usually broken, with light provided by a bare bulb hanging from the ceiling. When you finish bathing, you pull a plug from the tub, and water gushes across the floor seeking the drain somewhere across the room while you stand on a wooden platform to escape the soapy water. In the living room an old man lit Deodar logs in the fireplace. Their warmth and the smell of the cedar woodsmoke made life well worth living, and a nip of Scotch helped too. Several large, handsome, robinlike Blue Whistling Thrushes were singing in the courtyard or perched on the tile roof. They are a deep blue, spangled with pale blue dots.

Next morning we hired two minute horses and their boys as guides, and moved out to examine the countryside. Little bands of small birds flew through the oaks and pines that clothed the steep hillside. Almost at eye level several species of tits ganged together

*Kaleege Pheasants sailed into the valley below...*

much as the tufted titmice, chickadees, kinglets, and warblers do in America. With Ben's help I identified Great, Green-backed, and Black-throated Tits, as well as Chestnut-bellied Nuthatches and Bar-tailed Creepers. We found a Jungle Owlet hiding not three feet away in a low bush. Handsome, noisy Black-headed Jays and Blue Magpies were common.

In the rural countryside birding was excellent. Most species were new to me. I was fascinated watching an undulating flock of Long-tailed Minivets flash their brilliant colors in flight. Troops of White-throated Laughing Thrushes moved together near the ground, stiff-winged, gliding from bush to ground then to bush again, then gone. Stepping off the dirt road, I followed the calls of a Scimitar-billed Babbler. From the base of a low rhododendron thicket exploded a pair of White-crested Kaleege Pheasants. Cackling loudly, with a few flaps interspersed between long glides, they sailed into the deep valley below. I followed the two descending specks until they disappeared, then my eyes traveled upward to the distant range of blue mountains, the great Himalayan snow wall that seemed to stretch on forever. Well to the east was the crowning peak of Nanda Devi, soaring to an elevation of 25,645 feet.

Oddly enough this was the first time I had ever seen pheasants in their native habitat, though I was already very familiar with White-crested Kaleege Pheasants, having kept them at home for years. Few people realize that this ornate family of game birds is, with one exception, native only to Asia. (The exception is *Afropavo congensis*, the Congo Peafowl discovered in 1938.) The vast range of pheasants extends from Asia into Europe, stopping at the Caucasus Mountains. Only the well-known Ring-necked Pheasant and its various races

SPOTTED FORKTAIL

FROM THE SHAH JAHAN ALBUM — MUGHAL PERIOD 1605–1628
THE METROPOLITAN MUSEUM OF ART

have been successfully introduced outside the home range. The story goes that Alexander the Great introduced the common pheasant to Europe, and Julius Caesar brought it to England. It is a known fact that Benjamin Franklin's son-in-law introduced pheasants to America in 1790 by releasing several crateloads of these birds in New Jersey.

As I studied the spectacular landscape where the pheasants were flushed, through binoculars I saw that what had once been great sloping hillsides of pine and fir forests and rhododendron thickets were now reduced to exhausted farmland. Sparse, dry, and brown, the soil was almost untillable because of the steep incline. Everything in sight was overgrazed, overcut, and totally misused. Here and there a tall cedar or pine survived, though all the lower branches had been cut for firewood. Greenery started at a height above the reach of human hands, making the trees look like so many bottle brushes.

Along the roadside people and animals were laden with branches, grasses, and foliage, which they carried home for fuel or to patch their wattle and corrugated tin huts. Only on hillsides too steep to farm was vegetation still standing. No wonder the people are poor.

Apart from the usual cluster of small bazaars and shops, much of Mussorie consisted of small, mostly dilapidated hotels clinging to the hillsides. Many had fancy British names like Hyde Park, Connaught Castle, or Walnut Grove.

After three days in the high hill country, our Ambassador auto was partially repaired. We drove slowly down toward the great plains and on the way spent a day and a night at Dehra Dun, an old military community. Stopping by a small mountain stream, I was delighted to see two species of forktails — the Little and the Spotted Forktail. These graceful black-and-white members of the thrush family with decorative, scissorlike tails are found only by fast-moving streams, where they bob about the rocks and boulders as they hunt for insects.

After a night at New Delhi, we drove to Sultanpur, a waterfowl sanctuary about 100 miles to the southwest. Arriving about mid-morning at the shallow soda lake, we found the general scene rather depressing. Until very recently the lake had been the private hunting preserve of a maharajah. The surrounding fields were now colored tan and ochre. In every direction paired white oxen were hitched to crude wooden plows, tilling the soil, a practice unchanged for centuries.

Ben and I walked about the edges of the lake and the flats. It was now mid-November, but the bulk of the waterfowl had not yet arrived from their northern breeding grounds beyond the Himalayan range in Russia, China, and Tibet. The few thousand ducks already present were familiar Mallards, Gadwall, Shovelers, and Pintails. Mingled with these were European Teal, Wigeon, Spot-bills, White-eyes, Tufted Ducks, and Pochards. Herons, White Pelicans, cormorants, and several species of shorebirds were abundant. There was even a small group of Greater Flamingos feeding in the shallow mud. Toward sunset several hundred Common Cranes flew in from the surrounding grain fields. We could hear their glorious bugling calls all night long from the small sanctuary guesthouse situated on a rise overlooking the mile-wide lake.

Wattle and tin huts against the distant range

*Common Cranes over Sultanpur*

The next morning, while walking the lakeshore, I found three new birds of special interest — Isabline and Desert Wheatears and a solitary Bluethroat. These are all smallish members of the thrush family. Now in winter plumage, the Bluethroat had just a frosted suggestion of the handsome red, white, blue, and black throat pattern it sported when in breeding plumage.

Leaving Sultanpur we headed toward Siriska Sanctuary in Rajasthan. This too was once the domain and private hunting property of another maharajah. Today it is an eighty-square mile tiger preserve. The five-hour drive took us past open farmlands, but as evening approached we found ourselves driving through heavily forested rocky hills and deep ravines, some showing scattered oases of date palms. Clear, cool water tumbled over huge boulders and swirled about the ancient gnarled roots of fig and other forest trees. Black-faced Languar Monkeys roamed about in family groups, eating fruits and seeds, and turning over movable rocks as they looked for edible grubs, crickets, and centipedes.

As the sun sank behind the hills, cold air descended and settled into the valleys. Hordes of screeching Rose-ringed Parakeets flew by, headed for roosting trees. Numerous peafowl welcomed the oncoming night with their piercing cries. In such a setting I longed again to catch a glimpse of a tiger starting an evening hunt, coughing quietly as it slipped through the darkening forest hoping to come upon the fresh trail of a Sambar Deer.

We slipped on sweaters and parkas as we drove to our motel-like guest lodge. My room had a large cracked mirror, two chairs, two short beds to accommodate my six-foot-three frame, and the usual bare light bulb dangling from the ceiling. Army mess-type meals were served at one long table. But it all seemed adequate under the circumstances.

Halfway through the evening meal a group of about fifteen tourists, plus two guides, joined us at one long table. Their conversation soon turned to complaints — why had they seen so little wildlife during their five days in India? Most of these package-deal travelers had been to East Africa and seen the vast hordes of animals there. Why had they been so misinformed about Indian game? I marveled at the patience of the young British naturalist who was their tour leader. He took more rudeness from his clients than one should have to endure. I couldn't help blurting out that if they had done more homework before signing up, they would have known that today, in India, game is scarce, that the sight of one tiger is comparable to five prides of lion, or ten thousand wildebeests and zebra.

One night a group of us went out on a tiger watch. Wrapped in blankets (the temperature was in the fifties) we sat on the rooftop of an abandoned farmhouse. For five hours we looked down on a live tethered buffalo calf. Amid the screams and screeches of peafowl and parakeets our strict silence was occasionally interrupted by the stomach rumbles of unfed tiger-watchers. Anticipating the approaching tiger made the hours electric, but unfortunately no tiger appeared during our vigil.

Ben and I worked hard at our birding. I was pleased to find Painted Spurfowl, a beautifully colored, chickenlike bird spangled with white dots, and I quietly watched them scratching among the dried leaves on the ground. Tiny Jungle Bush Quail, half the size of our Bobwhite, took dust baths along the edge of a dirt road. White-browed Fantail Flycatchers hopped about the lower branches of shrubs, nervously exposing their exaggerated fantails very much the way our Redstarts do. Yellow-legged Green Pigeons were spotted feeding on the ripe fruit of fig trees. All of these were new to me.

Much of our birding took place along the roadside. We would drive to a likely area, pull the car off to the side, and walk. During the light hours there were always men, women, and children carrying small bundles of tied grass or sticks, walking single file, heading for home. The sticks would be turned into charcoal, and the grass fed to their domestic stock. Although we were in a park, this activity was unceasing. The pressure of people on the few remaining wilderness areas is continuous and tragic for all concerned.

On two evenings we rode in a truck over the same park roads. An alert Indian boy held a spotlight to pick up the many reflecting eyes in the blackness of the night forest. Nilgai (Blue Bull), India's largest antelope, were the most often seen. They are large, ungainly animals, somewhat horselike in build, with high withers and a low rump. The males are iron-gray with short conical horns. The females are brownish.

Spotted Chital or Axis Deer were abundant also. The males, with great racks of horns, are to me the most beautiful deer in the world. Both sexes and fawns are heavily spotted with white against a rich chestnut background. In size they are similar to our White-tailed Deer.

We saw a few Sambar, India's largest deer, with enormous elklike antlers. A big male may weigh 700 pounds. Most of these shy animals held their ground against the bright beam of our powerful light.

We also saw the tiny Four-horned Antelope, several wild pigs, and a jungle cat, probably the original ancestor of the house cat. Unlike the plains game of Africa, few of these animals are seen in the daytime. Only with great patience, luck, and lots of time can they be photographed at all.

On our last afternoon in Seriska we drove out of the park to a large lake in the midst of farming country. It was framed by gentle, treeless hills, with outcroppings of limestone rock.

Well to the west, on a limestone ridge boldly silhouetted against the setting sun, were the ruins of an ancient Moghul fort. The crum-

*House Crow and inlay work – Agra*

bling ramparts and walls were green with moss and ferns. Cackling calls were heard, and high above the fort came skeins of Bar-headed Geese. Several hundred gracefully circled the lake two or three times, then came in to land on the shore where there was green grass. The scene reminded me of so many of Sir Peter Scott's earlier paintings of hills, a distant castle, the setting sun, and the long wavering lines of geese.

These attractive Bar-headed Geese breed in the Tibetan highlands and winter in the Indian plains. They are still abundant despite being heavily hunted by the people of Tibet and neighboring countries.

We returned to New Delhi and the good creature comforts. All of her life my stepmother, Virginia Moseley, had wanted a firsthand glimpse of India. This present trip provided the opportunity. She joined me at the Intercontinental Hotel.

We did the sights of Delhi, motored to Agra, saw the Taj Mahal and Bharatpur sanctuary. Then we took a pleasant tour of the Rajahstan Maharajah palace circuit.

It is difficult to write about the Taj Mahal without seeming trite. I have seen it twice, and it is ever a marvel.

After an early dinner we taxied to the great, dark-red entrance gate. Walking through the high, weakly lit entrance portico, one finds oneself on a large stone terrace. A third of a mile away stands the Taj Mahal, an enormous, pale opalescent balloon, floating in space. One is aware of the silence. Human voices in the vast surrounding gardens become mere whispers. On my first visit a clear half-moon intensified the brightness of the marble and the blackness of the symmetrically planted cypress trees. Woodsmoke, with traces of spice, hugged the ground in a thin layer. How many others, like me, have looked upon it, speechless, then walked away and wept?

To me its vast size, Arabian-nights quality, and above all its superb proportions place it among the greatest man-made structures of all time. Chartres Cathedral, the Alhambra, the Palace of the Governors at Uxmal, even the Parthenon never had the same impact on me as my first view of the Taj Mahal.

Not more than thirty miles from Agra there is a naturalist's paradise, the waterfowl sanctuary known as Keoladeo Ghana, two miles from the town of Bharatpur. Here was once the private shooting preserve of the rulers of the old princely state of Bharatpur. Reservations had been made for us to spend three days at the maharajah's guesthouse, now opened to tourists.

Over the years fantastic shoots, or rather slaughters, had been held in this preserve, six square miles of impounded waters. At the junction of several large dikes is a small, wooded acacia tree park and a rather ornate brick-and-ironwork gazebo, where I imagine food and drink were formerly served to assembled hunters. Near this structure is a twenty-foot-long cement wall on which, listed chronologically, are the dates and numbers of birds killed. I photographed this wall to make sure I could believe my facts and figures.

On a shoot held for Lord Hardinge in December, 1914, 4,062 ducks were killed by 49 guns. For Lord Chemsford in November, 1916, 4,206 were killed by 50 guns. The greatest slaughter took place on

*Sarus Cranes*

November 12, 1938. A special hunt was organized for Lord Linlith-gow, then Viceroy of India, and with 41 guns present, 3,044 ducks were killed in the morning and 1,229 in the afternoon for a grand total of 4,273 ducks and 39 deer. One wonders what percentage of this wanton bag was put to use and what rotted away in the sun.

To me, with the possible exception of Kenya's Lake Nakuru, the sanctuary of Keoladeo Ghana offers the most spectacular show of waterbirds on earth. The sanctuary varies in size according to rainfall and the amount of water released by the local irrigation authorities. A series of large water impoundments connected by a network of crisscrossing dikes constitutes the sanctuary. Some of these tree-bordered dikes can be driven by car, while others are too narrow or come to a dead end. Poling in a flat-bottomed boat is the best way to get around the larger lakes. Now, in late November, the bird show would have been hard to beat. Sixteen species of migrant ducks, two kinds of geese, pelicans, and cranes had just arrived, and late-nesters like Spoonbills, Open-billed and Painted Storks were still feeding their young.

On our first afternoon we walked a mile or two along one bank. I saw the rare Siberian White Cranes, six adults with two brownish young. The next day we counted thirty-five scattered about in family or bachelor groups over a large area. Among the world's rarest cranes, these handsome white birds, rather similar to our Whooping Cranes but smaller, with longer bills, had flown the 3,000 miles from their tundra nesting grounds in Siberia to winter in India. There is another wintering ground in China, but little is known about that area.

With them were many Sarus Cranes, dwarfing their smaller white relatives. Graylag Geese, oinking like the barnyard variety, were

Siberian Cranes

present in large numbers, feeding along with ducks, coot, moorhens, and grebes. Pheasant-tailed and Indian Jacanas on long spidery toes ran about lily pads and other floating vegetation. Long files of White Pelicans flew in military formation low over the tree-lined banks. There were Great and Little Egrets, and the shyer Pond and Purple Herons. Indian Darters swam about with only their reptilian necks showing above water, or were perched on a branch with wings spread to dry in the sun. Indian Shags (cormorants) in close groups of thousands swam together by the sluice gates, fishing in the incoming water.

With such a superabundance of waterfowl it was to be expected that bird predators would also be in evidence to feed on the sick and dying. One morning, through binoculars, I watched two superb adult White-tailed Eagles fly quite near. One checked itself in flight, swooped down to the water, grabbed a coot, then flew to a dead tree to eat its prey. Imperial and Greater Spotted Eagles were often seen standing on the crest of a narrow bank, feeding on the carcasses of a waterfowl, a ring of plucked feathers surrounding them.

A pair of enormous Pallas Sea Eagles had a large nest atop a tall green tree in the middle of a pond. One or both of them were always nearby. The second day I counted seven species of eagles — Steppe, White-tailed, Greater Spotted, Imperial, Pallas, Tawny, and Crested Serpent Eagles. I doubt if even the African plains, with their exciting numbers of birds of prey, could top this display.

Armed with a Leicaflex camera and 400-mm lens, I rented a boat and a local poler. Quietly cruising the borders of the nesting rookeries, I exposed several rolls of film on White Spoonbills and Painted Storks. They allowed close approach and stood on their nests with wings open to shield their naked young from the sun's hot rays. A photographer could not have asked for better subjects. Several weeks later, when the processed film was returned to me, I found almost every frame badly overexposed. Though I had checked my light meter often, I had not taken into account the powerful light reflection from the glassy water.

The present maharajah still retains the right to hold shoots in the sanctuary, but I was told that he is very conservation-minded and that he admires and is advised by Salim Ali, India's foremost ornithologist. The maharajah has fought to convince the irrigation authorities of the importance of keeping the right amount of water in the ponds. Success or failure of a breeding season depends on it. These tens of thousands of storks, ibis, herons, and waterfowl require enormous amounts of food for themselves and their young during the summer months. This can be produced only when the water is at the right depth to insure the growth of plant life, microorganisms, and small fish. The water that supplies the sanctuary travels many miles through a great ditch, and local agricultural demand for it is staggering. During dry periods, as when the monsoons fail, Bharatpur finds itself in a precarious position.

Another increasingly serious problem is the hordes of cattle that are led into the sanctuary daily to graze on the grassy banks. They wade belly deep in the water and eat all aquatic plants within reach. Their sharp hooves can turn once-green banks into powdery dust.

Pelican and Coot

These three-and-a-half weeks in India were more than interesting, and far exceeded my expectations. I had become familiar with nearly two hundred Indian bird species, all new to me. Arriving home in early December I found myself walking a bit straighter, far better able to face the one thousand bird skins lined up in neat rows in steel cabinets. It was good to return to painting again.

Anhinga— Keoladeo Ghana Sanctuary

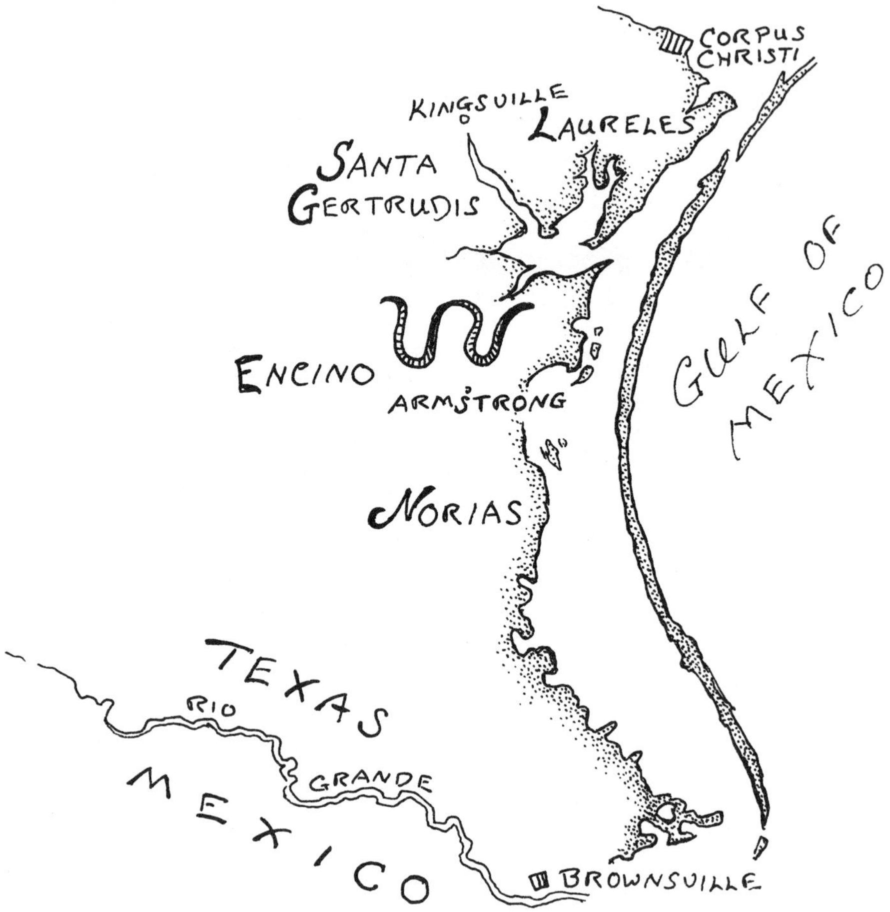
CORPUS CHRISTI
KINGSVILLE
LAURELES
SANTA GERTRUDIS
ENCINO
ARMSTRONG
NORIAS
GULF OF MEXICO
TEXAS
RIO GRANDE
MEXICO
BROWNSVILLE

# The King Ranch

IN JANUARY, 1974, I spent six days at the King Ranch, Texas, as guest of Robert T. Kleberg, Jr., baronial cattleman better known as "Mr. Bob" to the 15,000 people employed in this vast family empire. Comprising 400 square miles, it is larger than the State of Rhode Island. The interesting birdlife of the ranch, the unique quail hunting, and the opportunity to meet one of America's last land barons was something I looked forward to.

My invitation came through Gertie Legendre, a close friend of Bob Kleberg. I polished up my 20-gauge Griffin and Howe and packed a rather disreputable assortment of hunting clothes.

At the Houston airport a King Ranch jet was waiting for three ladies — Gertrude Legendre, Nancy Lancaster, Lillian Phipps — and me. We settled ourselves into large leather chairs and were offered a cooling drink as the door closed. The jet took off with a soft whisper, and forty-five minutes later we landed at Kingsville, scattering two large flocks of wild turkeys from the runway in the process.

Bob Kleberg was pacing the cement near a hangar as we disembarked. He was most anxious to take Lillian Phipps immediately to his racing stables and show her his lineup of thoroughbreds. At seventy-eight years of age he was a handsome man, ruddy-faced, with piercing eyes that flashed like an eagle's under a well-worn Stetson.

We drove perhaps ten miles to the stables, where everything was in prime condition, with freshly painted buildings and neat white fences.

The best I can do is admire horseflesh from afar, and I am also smart enough to keep my mouth shut in the presence of topnotch stable owners. I walked at a discreet distance behind Phipps and Kleberg and watched as Mexican stable boys led the beautiful animals from their stalls. From the conversation I gathered that this once-famous stable had fallen on nonproductive times. In better days two of Kleberg's horses, Assault and Middleground, had won the Kentucky Derby. Assault went on to win the Triple Crown in 1946 — the Derby, the Preakness, and the Belmont Stakes.

It was near lunchtime, so we left the stables and drove to Kleberg's unassuming seven-room house. One could tell at a glance that this was his favorite home. The chairs were well worn and comfortable. Every inch of wall space was covered with photographs of family, friends, dogs, horses, and cattle. A stone's throw away stood the large, three-storied, turreted family hacienda. I gathered that this was still used for entertaining large groups and for formal gatherings.

Seated at the lunch table, I addressed my host as Mr. Kleberg. In a rather severe tone he let me know that henceforth, if he and I were to get along, he would be called Bob. This I did for the remainder of the visit, but I don't believe he ever knew my first, middle, or even last name.

The history of the King Ranch and Bob Kleberg is fabulous and unique in America. Besides King Ranch, Inc., with its 960,000 acres of cattle and oil lands in Texas, Kleberg and Company own and operate 11.5 million acres abroad. Most of this acreage is in Australia, with lesser holdings in Venezuela, Brazil, Argentina, Spain, and Morocco. Another ranch in Cuba, with some of his finest Santa Gertrudis cattle, was confiscated by Castro.

As he often reiterated, Kleberg's main interest was cattle. Vast reserves of oil, leased to Humble Oil Company (now Exxon), were producing 15 to 18 million dollars annually for the ranch treasury. This was considered extra cash to be used in land clearing and cattle improvement at home or on overseas ranches. Kleberg once said: "We operated the ranch for eighty-five years without oil. When the oil money came in, we put it back into cattle. Cattle-raising is our business, and it will be our business long after the oil is gone."

I was amazed at his complete lack of interest in saving any natural habitat, and his obsession with transforming as much of the world as he could into pastureland.

Kleberg thought, lived, and dreamed cattle. Between 1916 and 1940, having suffered through many cattle-killing droughts, with perseverance and knowledge, he was solely responsible for the development of a new breed. His Santa Gertrudis were the first breed ever to be recognized as emanating from the Western Hemisphere. These large, handsome, cherry-red cattle were the result of crossing European Shorthorn with the heat-resistant Indian Brahmin cattle. Once he had proved the excellence of the Santa Gertrudis, he turned his interests to the development of new grasses able to withstand the rigors of the Texas plains and climate. Then he focused on improving the quarter horse, those wonderful working cow ponies essential to the management and handling of large herds of cattle. Many of these horses were shipped to ranches around the world. Some of the finest specimens sold for $25,000. These horses, some cattlemen say, "can start fast, turn on a dime, and give you back nine cents change."

Robert Justen Kleberg was born in Corpus Christi on May 29, 1896, and became a rancher by inheritance. His father acquired the King Ranch through his marriage to Alice King, the youngest daughter of Richard King, a riverboat captain who had founded the ranch in 1853. Richard King originally bought 54,000 acres south of Corpus Christi from the Santa Gertrudis grant, formerly a Spanish holding. Today this empire is divided into four main blocks — Santa Gertrudis, Laureles, Encino, and Norias, the southernmost area. I have read that from the extreme northern holding to the coastal plain, a distance of over 75 miles, there is a month's seasonal difference. Norias, with its rambling, almost motelish one-story, Spanish-style ranch house, was our residence.

After that first lunch we were driven about a small section of Norias, a vast domain in itself. The countryside was open and in certain areas had a slight roll to it. Scattered wooded patches were mainly scrub live oak, but the bulk of the land was pasture, now tawny brown and bordered by mesquite hedgerows. Everywhere were metal windmills, some abandoned and rusting, others active

*... long wavering lines of ducks and geese ...*

and pumping water into cement cisterns for cattle. A few natural ponds were bordered with cattail, willow, or cottonwood.

We passed through numerous bumper gates that divided the fenced cattle lands. When the car hits the right section of these large double metal gates, a balance weight automatically opens and shuts the gates.

Each time our two-car caravan would stop, Kleberg's ever-present Mexican servant, Arturo Barrientez, would jump out, open the back of the car, and offer us everything in the way of liquid refreshment, from a Dr. Pepper to Dom Perignon champagne.

We were assigned rooms at Norias, and after unpacking and bathing, we assembled in the big living room before dinner. Two more guests, the Robert Gerrys, had just arrived, and Kleberg's two attractive granddaughters, Emory and Tina Alexander, made their appearance.

The big Spanish-style living room was informal and comfortable. An enormous fireplace dominated one end of the room. At the other was a great round table on which were loaded cattle and horse periodicals and well-worn photograph albums of the highlights of Kleberg's career. The walls held several African antelope heads, two longhorn racks of extreme length, two excellent contemporary watercolors of racing stable life by Henry Kohler, and an autographed photograph of Great Britain's Queen Mother — not far from the photograph of a prize bull.

Since our host refused to eat early, the cocktail hour, I was to find, could continue until ten or even later. Seventy-eight years of hard work, hard living in a tough climate, and, more recently, the loss of a devoted wife had taken their toll on Bob Kleberg. When evening came the dynamic, driving cowboy was exhausted. He enjoyed his company and guests, but one felt he was happier out of doors in the open expanses of his empire.

Prior to breakfast several of the finest quarter-horses in the stable were paraded on the front lawn for inspection and the delight of everyone.

I particularly enjoyed the big breakfasts — eggs, bacon, fried tomatoes, pancakes, and exceptionally delicious sausages made from Nilgai Antelope.

Several types of antelope and deer had been introduced into Norias. A few African Impala and Indian Axis deer were barely holding their own, but not so the large Indian Nilgai or Blue Bull. Their numbers had built up into the hundreds until a severe winter cut them back. However, by 1974 their numbers had again increased enough to allow cropping — hence the Nilgai sausages.

Every morning after breakfast there was an hour's wait before we departed for the quail country. I would walk about the ranch compound birding.

Green Jays were common about the larger trees near the ranch house. These are beautifully colored, a bold combination of chartreuse green, black, and yellow. They animated the oak and pepper trees. I believe this must be the northernmost extent of their range in the United States. One lone Kiskadee Flycatcher sat on a dead branch above a ditch stream, waiting to pick up a minnow or insect. The large Cactus Wrens, Black-crested Titmice, wintering Bullock's Orioles, and flocks of Lesser Goldfinches were evident.

We left the house around 10:30 in two open cars, especially fitted for quail hunting. Gun racks were mounted on the front fenders, canvas-covered seats were raised for better viewing. Behind the back seat was an open trunk that held individually marked metal shell boxes and refreshment coolers. Following us were two trucks fitted with oversized tires that enabled them to go anywhere. They carried the dogs and their handlers.

... *The dogs wore ... rubber boots ...*

We drove on good paved roads for about ten miles. Then the safari turned into a vast weedy pasture. The dogs wore specially fitted rubber boots taped at midleg with adhesive. These were necessary, as the ground was littered with inch-long cactus spines, giant sandspurs, and other cutting weed-seed cases. Without their boots the dogs would soon have lacerated pads and become helpless. As it was, turned loose in the field, they were easily kept track of by the audible flop-flop of their boots as they ran about.

Within minutes the dogs would be on point. As one walked up to them, another undiscovered covey often would burst, like the explosion of a hand grenade, at one's feet. I never knew so many Bobwhite Quail existed in the world.

I must admit that quail shooting, Texas-style, was wild and woolly, especially to one who had always been extremely careful in handling

*Green Jays were common. . . .*

a gun in the field. Anything was permissible — shooting birds from the car, over the car, shooting to the left, right, in front of you or behind. No Alphonse-Gaston routine here. What made the hunt unique was that when coveys rose, they flew hardly more than 300 feet at most. It was remarkably easy to pursue singles.

Limits were never mentioned, and on our first day in the field, with seven guns, good, bad, or indifferent, the total bag was 240 birds. Until that day I had never reached my limit. To be honest, the opportunity to exceed the limit had never before been presented.

The percentage of birds killed in contrast to those that survived convinced me that no harm had been done to their numbers whatsoever. White rings of covey droppings littered the fields, a good indication of their amazing numbers.

Holding a dead bird in my hand, I noticed that it was slightly smaller than the Carolina Bobwhite, and the black breast markings were wider and darker. There are many races of Bobwhite in North America and Mexico, and, as a rule, the farther north one goes, the larger they tend to be.

The ground underfoot was pockmarked and honeycombed with rodent burrows. Overhead, large hawks of several species circled in numbers. Redtails were the commonest, followed by Harris's — a dark Buteo with rufous "trousers" and a black-and-white tail — and finally, the rather scarce, pale Sennett's White-tailed Hawk. Smallish kestrels and White-tailed Kites hovered over the fields, trying to pick up the motion of a rodent or insect below. When the sun was low, buffy Short-eared Owls on velvet wings quartered the fields like large nighthawks. Several members of our hunting party came upon mammoth Diamond-back Rattlesnakes, which were immediately shot. Invariably these snakes were found coiled about the base of a cactus pear at a rodent hillock waiting for a tenant to appear.

I found this extraordinary interrelationship between hawks, rodents, snakes, and quail fascinating. Each seemed to benefit from the other's presence. Of course, to the ranch hands the quail was the hero, everything else the enemy. Hawks most certainly do kill quail, as numerous scattered feather clumps testified, but they must have preferred rodents as a diet, for never in my life have I seen native quail so abundant. They were probably at the peak of their abundant phase.

Upon our arrival at the prearranged site for lunch we would find tarpaulin windbreakers already in place. Tables were prepared, and all manner of refreshments were cooling on ice. Approaching these picnic sites from afar, I felt like a member of an Arab sheik's gathering in the desert.

On our way to one picnic rendezvous, Kleberg's eagle eye spotted a young unaltered bull among many steers and cows. He gave a quick order, and a cowhand jumped on the radiator of our car, lasso in hand. After a short, zigzagging chase, the bull was roped and castrated on the spot. Half an hour later fried prairie oysters were served as appetizers as we drank cold Mexican beer. I found this local delicacy very good, tasting rather like sweetbreads. The prairie oysters, like cooked rattlesnake or chocolate-covered ants served elsewhere, are often lavished mainly for shock effect on the visiting dude.

Lunches consisted largely of local ranch game — venison, Nilgai Antelope, Javelina (wild pig), and duck, served up in hash or stew. One warm day a large, clear lucite bowl was passed around; it contained whole cold quail, sliced cucumbers, peas and celery, all mixed in a delicious vinaigrette sauce. Our host always had a small dish of chopped green chili peppers before him at mealtimes. It was far too hot to be left carelessly on the table, within easy reach of those with unsuspecting palates.

Game and wildlife were common ground on which Bob Kleberg and I could talk with ease. As his guest I was in no position to remind him of how much of the natural world he had destroyed. The thousands of acres of mesquite wilderness that once knew the wolf, ocelot, and even the jaguar had completely vanished under the blades of bulldozers. If a bird or animal could not adjust to cattle pasture, it disappeared. There was a gain of sorts, but at the loss of

... We came across Nilgai antelope ...

much wildlife. Commodity production seemed to me much over-done.

Before leaving for the quail hunt one morning, Bob summoned his top naturalist and biologist, Bill Kiel. I had been anxious to meet him, so he was asked to join us for lunch in the fields. We got along well and had a long walk together while everyone else took a post-lunch siesta.

He spoke freely on ecology and the wildlife situation on the ranch, confessing that all he could do was try to keep the ranch as healthy and well balanced as possible. He mentioned the difficulty of preventing cowboys and other ranchmen from killing hawks, an inborn part of their lifestyle.

... car lights ... flushed Paraques...

*... glorious bugling notes of Sandhill Cranes ...*

As we walked around the edge of a large, diked cattle pond, Wilson's Snipe jumped at our feet. On this same pond there were the three American teal — Greenwing, Bluewing, and Cinnamon — who swam away through brown aquatic weeds. A Vermilion Flycatcher, a fiery dot, perched on the tip of a dead branch. In his position as ranch biologist, it was difficult for Kiel to be unbiased, but I was impressed with his fairness. He did his best to convince me that the King Ranch, though ecologically much altered, was, as a whole, still a wildlife paradise.

As we headed home after the shoot, geese and ducks flew toward the bays of the Gulf Coast. Blue Geese and Lesser Snows, and a few skeins of White-fronts passed overhead, but most prominent were long, waving lines of big Canadas. Lesser Canadas, which are small facsimiles of their bigger relatives, were easily identified by their shorter necks and higher-pitched barking calls.

The marvelous bugling notes of Sandhill Cranes were heard long before the birds appeared to join the evening spectacle. Lark Buntings flew in tight flocks and settled into low bushes for the night. At this midwinter season the striking black-and-white males were in a drab sparrowlike plumage, but still showed their white wing patches. Cardinals and their rather similar parrot-billed relatives, the Pyrrhuloxias, whistled and chipped in the hedgerows along the side of the road.

In the open car, well bundled against the cold, with the west splashed in a red afterglow, I saw the stars emerge. After dark the car lights revealed Paraques, Mexican whippoorwill relatives, who, when in flight, flashed their startling white wing and tail patches.

On the fourth day we drove in a new direction, to the southeast sector of the Norias, to the tidal Gulf marshes near the inland waterway. This was altogether different terrain, mostly open, native prairie land. Long-billed Curlews flushed before the car, showing cinnamon underwing feathers and very long, thin, graceful bills. Cattail-bordered ponds in low places abounded with Pintail and Redhead ducks. The country seemed wilder, with less evidence of cattle and pasture management. Large White-tailed Deer were abundant. Some of their racks were indeed noble.

At midmorning we stopped at a lovely glade of live oaks, their windswept branches covered with Resurrection Ferns and banners of Spanish moss. In the sun-dappled grass was a small hill of bleached antlers. This spot had been, for many years, a tenting area where the Klebergs and their friends often camped. Deer that had been shot were hung, butchered, skinned on the spot, and their antlers added to the pile.

Here, too, we came across several Nilgai Antelope. When motionless, they are difficult to see, since they blend so perfectly with the twisted branches and bush around them. Kleberg invited me to shoot one, but I declined. Thinking back on my early hunting days in Africa, I dreaded the rifle's crack and the following "thunk" of a bullet hitting flesh. My animal-shooting days were behind me.

Large flocks of wild turkeys appeared near the road, searching in the fallen leaves for acorns. Standing in the shade, they seemed all black, but when they stepped into the sunshine, their sombre colors

*... large flocks of Wild Turkeys ...*

shone and smouldered like coals in a fire. Two toms were shot from the car by our party. Then Bob Kleberg spotted two Javelinas rooting in a damp thicket. To show the ladies that his eagle eye and aim were steady as ever, he aimed a revolver and killed them neatly.

We spent most of the day in the hunting cars and drove vast distances. My car companions were Nancy Lancaster, Emory and Tina Alexander, and our ranch hand driver, Lavoy Durham, who was the son of the manager of Norias. In his twenties, Lavoy was tall and lanky, with a magnificent Texas drawl. Nancy Lancaster, in her late seventies, very British, was handsome and talkative. The two of them made an odd couple as they sat together in the front seat and needled each other about accents and grammar. When Nancy cast her eye on his well-worn, ten-gallon hat, it was obvious that she coveted it. But since it was given to Lavoy by the great man himself, nothing short of a tornado would have made him part with it. Nancy Lancaster was insistent, but ultimately accepted it as a lost cause.

On our last day at the King Ranch we drove to a complex of fence junctions, where holding pens widened into one large central corral. Dust billowed up from the area like a storm cloud. A few cars were parked, and *vaqueros* (Tex-Mex cowboys) on horseback rode about. This was a routine roundup, an almost daily occurrence somewhere on the ranch.

In a world of dust, galloping hooves, and the whooping and hollering of ranch hands, we watched the show from the tops of our cars. Bob Kleberg left his car, put on white leather chaps, climbed onto a quarter horse, and rode into a milling, moaning herd of some 600 cattle. Scrutinizing the animals, he cut a calf from its mother, since these young males were now too old to be with the cows. Riders and horses were superb, able to stop abruptly and turn left or right at hellish speed. Within seconds they could single out a calf and keep it from returning to the main herd. Spinning lariats roped the animals, who were then bulldogged to the ground. Here they were branded, castrated, inoculated, and dabbed with white paint for future iden- tification. It was an exciting show, little changed from the days portrayed by Charles Russell, Will James, and Frederic Remington.

After the roundup all hands lined up with tin plates for a groaning barbecue lunch and cold beer. Looking across the table at Kleberg's flushed, dusty face, streaked with sweat, the real secret of his power came to me. Here was a man who had won control and respect because he had never ordered another man to do a job, no matter how menial, that he was not able to do himself.

On our last evening at Norias ranch foreman Durham and his son Lavoy joined us for drinks in the big living room. Stetson in hand, pushing back his black hair, Lavoy approached Nancy Lancaster and shyly said, "Mrs. Lancaster, ma'am, I'd like for you to have my hat." Nancy was delighted and accepted his gift. She immediately stuck it on her head with an air of victory. Bob Kleberg had been sizing up the situation and consoled the young man. "Don't worry, Lavoy. I'll get you another."

Bob Kleberg died later that year, on October 13, 1974. I've often wondered if Lavoy Durham ever got another hat — not any old ten-gallon hat, but one given him by the great man himself.

*Roundup time on the King Ranch*

ELLESMERE IS.

79.6°N

GREENLAND

*- ICE THICKNESS 11,190'

DEVON IS.

THULE AIR BASE

UPERNAVIK

LANCASTER SOUND

BAFFIN BAY

IGDLORSSUIT

POND INLET

DISKO

JAKOBSHAVN

HOLSTEINSBORG

BAFFIN ISLAND

SONDRE STROMFJORD

CANADA

GODTHAB

NARSSARSSUAQ

DAVIS STRAIT

HUDSON STRAIT

CAPE FAREWELL

# Greenland Cruise - Eskimos and Polar Bears

My THIRD ADVENTURE to the arctic took place in July, 1974, when Devin Garrity and I sailed on the Lindblad *Explorer* from New York. We cruised 5,929 nautical miles and made 33 anchorages along the west coast of Greenland, then on the Canadian side, Ellesmere, Devon, and Baffin Islands. Ellesmere Island, an enormous area of mountains, glaciers, and windswept rocky valleys is the closest land to the actual North Pole. Captain Nilsson headed the ship into Kennedy Channel to a position farther north than any cruise ship had ever penetrated. We were stopped at latitude 79.7° by a fifty-foot wall of ice that may have continued unbroken to the pole itself. The captain carefully navigated the ship into bays and fjords where few if any ships had ever anchored. Having a double-hulled ice cutting bow we were capable of moving with ease through fields of ice three feet thick.

When we looked over the people who would be our shipmates for a month, the outlook seemed rather grim. Many passengers seemed bored already, and a large group of Japanese (twenty in all) spoke no English. A startling man, short, stout, and full-bearded — he resembled Karl Marx or a disgruntled Santa Claus — appeared on deck. Accompanying him were three blond "Lolitas" and a male companion, billed as his doctor and photographer. The talk on board soon had it that the bearded character was one of Denmark's richest citizens, a porno king, who also owned many hotels and travel agencies. One of his unhappy little girls, wearing green nail polish and clutching a stuffed toy dog, constantly snapped a yo-yo. After we arrived in Greenland, she evidently displeased her master, for she vanished from the scene, being returned to Denmark by helicopter and jet. Her place was taken quickly by a new model. Whenever we were on shore all passengers were asked to wear their red jackets (for visual safety reasons), but this colorful Dane firmly insisted on being dressed in a sable coat and sable hat. During the nightly after-dinner lecture, just as the speaker began his talk, his troop would rise at a given signal and stomp from the lecture room amid boos from the audience. To no one's surprise, this exotic character left the ship with his flock halfway through the month's cruise and flew home.

On the way north we had stopped briefly on the French-owned island of St. Pierre, which hugs the south coast of Newfoundland. Its much larger sister island, Miquelon, is sparsely populated, with no

fishing boat at St. Pierre

*... Ravens croaked overhead ...*

more than 700 inhabitants. Miquelon's claim to fame rests on her treacherous westerly shoals. Together with Nova Scotia's Sable Island, these constitute the most notorious ship graveyards in the Atlantic. A research team from the National Geographic Society cites a total of 676 sizable ships that have foundered off Miquelon since 1816.

The tricolor of France was most apparent in the quiet little fishing village of St. Pierre. Names like Rue Marechal Foch and Place General de Gaulle left no doubt as to the ownership of the island. The simple, brightly painted houses with their lace-curtained windows seemed designed to defy the dreariness of the dark winter days.

Following a tip from *Gourmet* magazine, we found table space at Chez Dutins, a small, private home-restaurant. Two rooms held four family-size tables. Madame was working in the kitchen while her daughter served our group a marvelous Brittany-style five-course meal with a paté maison, good homemade bread, and carafes of red wine. The entrée, I well remember, was a *poulet chasseur*, chicken baked in white wine, tomato sauce, mushrooms, and ripe olives.

We climbed the hill behind the town of St. Pierre, an area of large granite boulders and stunted spruce and alders, and walked along a boggy stream. Low-growing Labrador Tea and Dwarf Dogwood were both in full bloom. When the breeze died down, mosquitoes and black flies swarmed. We flushed a Least Sandpiper, who feigned a broken wing to try to lead us away from its nest. Fox Sparrows whistled their clear liquid songs, and nesting warblers (Yellow, Myrtle, Wilson's, and Redstarts), Winter Wrens, thrushes, pipits rounded out the list of passerine birds. Ravens croaked overhead, and as I walked back to the ship a Golden Eagle was seen.

Underway again and heading northeast we saw, far off along the western horizon, a line of icebergs moving southward, blown by strong winds and carried by sea currents. It was southeast of this same area, on a calm night in April, 1912, that the *Titanic* met her fate. On her maiden voyage, traveling at full speed toward New York, she struck an iceberg. The impact tore a 300-foot gash in her starboard side, and three hours later the great ship sank headfirst into the icy waters. There were 705 survivors, but about 1,502 lives were lost (the exact figure has never been resolved).

Among the survivors was my mother, who was returning from a year-long European honeymoon. She was then eighteen years old and five months pregnant. As teenagers my older brother Billy and I would beg her for stories connected with the disaster. She had little to tell. When she left the sinking ship, the full impact of the impending nightmare had not yet spread among the passengers. The *Titanic* was "unsinkable." Only those left on board during that last hour would realize the irony of that claim.

It was some two hours after the initial jolt of metal hitting ice that most of the ship's officers admitted to the extreme seriousness of the situation. Then the shocking fact became apparent — this superliner was fitted out with only enough lifeboats to accommodate a third of the passengers. With several women, my mother was helped into one of the few released boats. Bidding her farewell, her husband, Col. John Jacob Astor, assured her that this was just a precautionary measure. The "unsinkable" *Titanic* would soon be made safe. The two never met again. The *Carpathia*, a small Cunard passenger ship on a run to Trieste, Italy, picked up the *Titanic*'s distress signals and rushed to the scene. At dawn she rescued the few lifeboats bobbing about in the choppy sea. About one week later a search vessel from Halifax, Nova Scotia, found the body of Colonel Astor and others floating in the general area of the disaster. Fifteen hundred people had died, plunged from warmth, light, and gaiety to icy doom.

Daily life aboard a small cruise ship has many good and many bad aspects. Though all who wished to go ashore were taken as often as possible, much of the time was spent reading, chatting, napping, eating and drinking. The Lindblad *Explorer*, a 2500-ton, 250-foot-long ship, had accommodations for a full complement of 90 passengers. When the six o'clock cocktail hour struck, the gathering in the saloon was usually augmented by off-duty ship's officers. Even though there were passengers one might like to have known better, one hesitated to leave a seat, because it was snapped up at once. We tended to divide into quite separate groups.

Cruising toward southern Greenland for the next three days, strong winds and heavy seas kept many of the passengers below in their cabins. The ship was heading into a world of icebergs. Radar and crew members on the bridge scanned the horizon twenty-four hours a day. I was intrigued by the way in which the navy has classified icebergs by size: Floating bits are called brash ice; greyhound-bus size are growlers; house-size are bergy-bits; and only the big ones are true icebergs.

Our first view of the southern tip of Greenland presented a jagged line of mountains, barely visible beyond the icebergs and ice fields. Taking notes, one comes up with some startling facts and figures about Greenland. Four times the size of France, it is the largest island in the world, although many geologists now believe it to be three or more islands covered over by one massive ice dome. Over 800,000 square miles in area, 600,000 of these compose the ice cap, which averages 5,000 feet in thickness and at some places is 11,000 feet thick. The distance between its northernmost point, Cape Morris Jesup, and its southernmost tip, Cape Farewell, is 1,660 miles. Temperatures in the north can reach 95 degrees below zero F. In the south (nicknamed the banana belt) 80 degrees above is not uncommon during the short summer.

It is now a thousand years since the first Europeans (Norsemen) arrived in the south of Greenland and settled there. Today 45,000 people are scattered along its 25,000 miles of coast — 38,000 of these are Eskimos and 7,000 are Danes. Greenland is something of a weight around the neck of its mother country, Denmark. It costs the average Dane $600 a year to support this giant colony, but it is hoped that the fishing industry and mineral deposits will eventually pay off.

Climbing a gentle hillside slope I noticed Greenland's only trees — birch and willow hugging the ground so closely that they are hardly recognized. Colorful wildflowers were easier to see and more widespread. I was amazed to find that my first identifiable flower on Greenland soil was a small spiked white orchid (*Leucorchis albida*). Drifts of purple Dwarf Fireweed and Cotton Grass favored wet spots, while, farther up the slopes, they were replaced by nodding blue harebells, Yellow Poppies, Lousewort, and minute Blue Gentians.

Upland birding was rather limited. Numerous ptarmigan feathers and droppings indicated that this arctic grouse was nearby and abundant. A few ravens were overhead, gliding gracefully and swooping about the high rocky crags. Lapland Longspurs and Snow Buntings sang from lichen-covered rocks, or flew past, their bills packed with insects for young. Greenland Wheatears, larger than their European counterparts, with flashy white rumps, were easy to spot as they flew from boulder to boulder. Sparrowlike Redpolls, splashed with raspberry on crown and chest — these made up my entire small-bird list here.

The village landing at Qagssiarssuk was the site of Greenland's first Nordic settlement (A.D. 982) with its one tiny Christian church. In a lush green field we walked about the simple reddish sandstone ruins of this ancient Norse community, along with grazing sheep. The odd-shaped place of worship, we were told, was commissioned by the wife of Eric the Red. The foundation of the church is still clearly visible. It measures eight feet square and could hold 25 worshipers if packed like sardines.

Eskimos were living and farming near the stone ruins. Their plywood and tarpaper shacks were surrounded by broken boxes, plastic junk, rusted bedsprings, tin cans, worn tractor tires, and the remains of fish. This was a mere preview of the garbage and litter we

*... orchids and hare bells ...*

were to encounter in villages farther north. I daresay that the inhabitants feel that as everything is covered with snow nine months out of twelve, why bother to hide it. A few small garden patches had potatoes, now in bloom, root vegetables, and greens. Chickens, pigeons, even a few turkeys were scratching about. Black-haired, ruddy-cheeked children, some without shirts, but all wearing blue jeans and rubber boots, played in the warm sunshine. Higher up on the slope of a hill another Eskimo was plowing a field behind a team of workhorses.

Godthab is Greenland's capital and largest city. Walking about the town, I was aware of the humming and clanging of pneumatic drills, earth-movers, and rumbling dynamite blasts. Ultramodern offices, supermarkets, complete with turnstiles, hair sprays, and deodorants, banks and apartment buildings were springing up everywhere.

The overall impression made by the town was colorless and stark. The only spots of brightness were the numerous small crimson trawlers clustered together in the harbor. The population in 1974 was about 8,000, most of whom were involved with the fish and shrimp industry. We were given a tour of the fish processing and packaging plant and I saw equipment as modern as that anywhere in the world. Machinery was of spotless stainless steel. Eskimo workers were dressed in immaculate white uniforms and black rubber boots. The fish were fileted, boxed, and, we were told, shipped to Nigeria. Though caught now in two worlds, many Godthab Eskimos still hunt at sea with harpoon and gun for seal, whale, seabirds and, of course, fish — a pattern of living that will be difficult to change.

Walking about the outskirts of Godthab I spotted a strange white hill, which turned out to be a jumble of thousands of intertwined

Caribou skull

*... near Igdlorssuit ...*

reindeer antlers. The owner explained that all of these horns would be shipped to Hong Kong, where they would be ground into powder and sold as an aphrodisiac.

A small wood-frame museum near the sea exhibited ivory tupilaks and soapstone carvings, wonderfully wrought kayaks, Narwhal horns, and beaded sealskin costumes. The most memorable art objects were birdskin blankets, with circular, kaleidoscopic designs created from loon and eider skins, striking in color, design, and craftsmanship.

Igdlorssuit, north of Disko Bay, is 400 miles above the Arctic Circle, and it was in this primitive village during the 1930s that the famous American artist, Rockwell Kent, spent a year sketching and painting Eskimos and recording their culture. Kent's leftist politics made him

*munes on a dog sled*

unpopular during the prewar era and caused him to become an expatriot. Many of his finest works were left to the Hermitage collection in Leningrad.

Stepping ashore on Igdlorssuit's pebble beach, we were greeted by a dozen husky dogs gnawing and fighting over the enormous backbone and skull of a beached Fin Whale. One dog, completely hidden except for a protruding tail, was working within the skull itself. We had stepped into a world of dogs. They were everywhere, lying about the shore, resting between the plywood shacks, some even stretched out asleep on the roof of the one small church. All were shedding their heavy winter coats and looked a sorry lot. Whereas humans in the village numbered about a hundred, there were at least five dogs to very man, woman, and child.

The relationship between dog and Eskimo is remarkable. Seldom is "man's best friend" petted, pampered, or shown any affection. Rather, they are eyed with suspicion and kept at bay. I saw a small child walking the stony beach slip and fall. Immediately dogs were on top of her, and only the stone-throwing gesture of an adult nearby held off the snarling animals. Several times as a suspicious-looking husky approached I found the stone-throwing gesture comforting and effective. Apart from venereal disease and alcoholism, dog bite is one of the commonest maladies contended with by the few Greenland hospitals. In the winter, when the husky still provides the only means of transportation, he is well fed, well exercised, thickly furred, and handsome. He serves his purpose.

Except for the larger communities of Godthab, Holsteinborg, and Jakobshavn, there is a sameness to the coastal villages in Greenland. Small, brightly painted shacks perch precariously among great granite boulders. Always within sight are complexes of wooden racks supporting strips of drying cod, halibut, shark, whale, and blubber.

... Husky Dogs were everywhere ...

Much of this is fed to the hordes of dogs. Among the stretched sealskins drying in the air were dogskins curing in the same fashion. At one village hundreds of pounds of orange-brown blubber lay in heaps on the ground or draped across roofs, spilling over the eaves. A limited population of flies and bacterial action prevented this mess from smelling worse than it did.

After a night's cruise north from Jakobshavn in our ship's Zodiacs, we carefully cruised the edge of the spectacular Equip Sermia Glacier, situated at the end of a fjord, a high, jagged face protruding into the bay. Blue-green, cathedral-size chunks of ice broke away periodically with the deep boom of a cannon shot, then in slow motion vanished under water and reappeared as a floating iceberg. The resultant oncoming wave required careful maneuvering of our rubber boats.

I remember cliffside colonies of Glaucous and Iceland Gulls, two species I had never seen nesting before. Old-Squaw Ducks, surprised at the head of a fjord, circled in tight flocks, then flew past our boat to sea. Often heard were Red-throated Loons, in pairs overhead, giving their strange quacking calls.

When we walked the high tundra country, we flushed families of Rock Ptarmigans and a few nesting Purple Sandpipers. Both of these species would generally appear on the top of a boulder and watch us warily until we passed. Many small ponds and wet potholes were occupied by nesting Red-necked Phalaropes. The young would join their parents, swimming in tight circles and jabbing at invisible insects on the surface of the water. Everywhere in coastal Greenland I was conscious of the close proximity of the massive central ice cap, sometimes visible, spilling over into valleys, but more often seen at a distance like the icing on a mammoth cake.

Cruising northward from Upernavik in Greenland to Ellesmere Island in Canada, the calm seas of Baffin Bay looked alive with millions of tiny black-and-white Dovekies. These starling-size auks buzzed overhead in large flocks as they moved from their feeding ground to their nesting cliffs on the Greenland side of the bay. The oily dark seas were peppered with them, bobbing on the surface like corks. They dove ahead of our approaching bow when there was no breeze present, since their tiny wings were then unable to lift them in flight.

Equip Sermia Glacier

Zodiacs took us ashore at several places on Ellesmere and Devon Island. I was impressed with the rock formations and grandeur, colors, and sweep of the landscape, but most of all with the silence that only a total wilderness can give. Themes from the music of Sibelius often ran through my mind, evoked by the mood and vastness of our surroundings.

Ashore, somewhere on the coast of Ellesmere Island, on a gray sleety afternoon, I walked over tundra and hard-packed snowdrifts and stumbled on a lone Arctic Hare, mostly white and large as a hound dog. Since it had probably never seen a human before, it was very tame, often standing on its hind legs for a better view. Farther on I found a musk-ox skull, green with algae. Most of the large carcass bones lay nearby. There were Arctic Fox scats and numerous cross-hatched trails of caribou, but no other signs of living animals. Bright as jewelry in a Tiffany window were the tight clumps of blooming saxifrage that grew amongst stone and lichen. I made my first sighting of King Eider Ducks when a small flight came at me, suddenly flared, and then vanished in fog.

Rock Ptarmigan ... appeared
on top of a boulder ...

*Old-Squaw Ducks circled in tight flocks...*

One evening we were all turned loose on Devon Island to walk the delta area of a stream that flowed into a sheltered bay. The low midnight sun painted the great sandstone cliffs with every imaginable shade of purple, bronze, and gold.

Walking the borders of countless rivulets through beds of marsh marigolds, I flushed several pairs of nesting Baird's Sandpipers, some with newly hatched chicks. A flock of perhaps 30 Greater Snow Geese, now flightless because of summer molt, walked away and stumbled up steep tundra slopes. Through my binoculars I saw that two or three of the geese had golden goslings toddling behind, struggling and tumbling over the low plant life as they sought to keep up with their parents.

In the region of Devon Island and Lancaster Sound, the bays, fjords, and coves were still covered with ice. Here walrus, seal, and polar bear were evident. Generally, they were found not far from one another. When walrus sit on floes, they are easy to see from a great distance. Their broad dark backs and white, downward-pointing tusks clearly set them apart from smaller seals. They were exceedingly shy. If approached within 200 feet they would, in sudden panic, hump their great bulk over the ice floes, slip effortlessly into the water, and vanish.

Polar Bears are silent, handsome beasts. Dignified, aloof, and totally fearless of man, they move majestically in this, their natural world. All are a rather dirty cream color, and the males are huge, weighing up to 1,200 pounds. When the *Explorer*, breaking through three-foot ice, overtook them as they loped ahead of us, some would suddenly plunge into open, lead-gray water, then scramble back on to the ice farther ahead, turning occasionally to give us a disdainful look. We saw some of these bears twenty-five miles from land. When hunting seals, these creatures live on ice at an even greater distance from the coast. I have read that they do not hesitate to swim at an even pace as far as 100 miles in rough, open water when searching for better hunting grounds.

*... clumps of saxifrage ...*

*... a lone Arctic Hare ...*

Three seabirds of ethereal whiteness are to be seen at opposite ends of the earth — the Fairy Tern of the tropics, the Antarctic Snow Petrel, and the Ivory Gull of the arctic. Resting on an ice floe, Ivory Gulls in pristine plumage seem to turn everything about them gray by comparison. We saw them often, like camp followers, never far from bear, walrus, and seal. They scavenge by feeding on food scraps, sometimes even animal excrement.

One evening in the high arctic we had a picnic on heavy pack ice. There were bear tracks in the snow about us and Ivory Gulls wheeled overhead. Captain Nilsson brought the ship to a halt in four-foot ice, lowered the gangplank, and we were allowed to "land." On the ice the galley staff grilled steaks. Red wine and hot coffee flowed freely. In a flush of camaraderie, we shuffled and slid about the uneven glassy surface, like children released from school after the first cold had frozen the village pond. Our voices and laughter must have carried for miles.

An overnight run returned us again across Baffin Bay to Greenland. We cruised up Sondre Stromfjord 100 miles to the American Dewline Airbase. Here a chartered plane flew us the next day to Montreal and home.

That last evening, as the ship moved slowly into this spectacular fjord and the pale moon shone to port, we entered the most perfect of Wagnerian settings, a playground for Nordic gods and goddesses. Jet black mountains towered on both sides of the seaway, mist hung in the valleys, and ghostly icebergs slipped silently past, slowly drifting to the open sea.

*Polar Bears ... moved majestically ...*

GULF OF
MEXICO

MEXICO

ACAPULCO

GUATEMALA

TIKAL

PACIFIC

OCEAN

LIMA
PARACAS

PERU

COSTA
RICA

MT. IRAZÚ

COLÓN

PANAMA

SAN
JOSÉ

SOUTH
AMERICA

COCOS
IS.

# The American Tropics - Costa Rica, Tikal, and Condors

IN THE NORTHERN latitudes birdlife species are relatively few, the numbers correspondingly large, and the plumage often drab. In contrast, tropical birds are prolific in speciation and often brilliant in coloration. A vast range of habitats and altitude zones support a staggering variety of plant, insect, and bird life. The birder wishing to add glamour and numbers to his list can do no better than to start in tropical America. But do not delay, as, worldwide, 27 million acres of rain forests are being destroyed yearly, much of this in the Americas.

My first exposure to birding in tropical forests occurred in 1960 when I joined Devin Garrity on a business-pleasure tour of Central America. We were invited to visit Alexander F. Skutch, a Baltimore-born philosopher and professional botanist who had carved out a home for himself in the Costa Rican wilderness. Married to the daughter of an Englishman stationed in San José, he has become the world's top authority on Central American birds.

He met us at the El General bus stop in the central highlands and took us by jeep to his residence in the Costa Rican rain forest. There we met his shy, charming wife, and were shown our quarters in a small outbuilding. Entering the one-room shack, I was conscious of a loud buzzing sound and noticed, attached to the ceiling near the cot where I was to sleep, a huge gray paper nest crawling with blue-black hornets. Skutch apologized for the insects. Then he mentioned casually that vampire bats were sometimes about at night, assuring us, however, that they drew blood only from cattle and horses. I couldn't help observing that the two open windows had neither screens nor glass. I was even more dismayed when he handed me a small electric torch and suggested that we make a careful scrutiny of the trail to the outhouse. Apparently the Fer-de-lance had been seen traveling that path at night.

Shortly we joined our host for what proved to be a rather elaborate but meatless dinner. From subsequent conversations we learned that Skutch did not believe in killing creatures of any sort, even mosquitoes. He was a total vegetarian, and hornets, vampire bats, and Fer-de-lances were an accepted part of his ménage. His hatred of killing even extended indirectly to the predatory hawk — owl families for which he harbored a noticeable dislike and ignored in his studies. This deep feeling against killing had its ironic side. The Skutches kept chickens that ran wild about the yard, and during the normal course of events produced as many roosters as hens. The battles royal between the cocks would have delighted any aficionado of that ancient and bloody sport.

We survived our first night safely, and, early the next morning, Skutch led us through a nearby rain forest, where army ants were busily on the move. Manakins, numerous species of flycatchers, woodcreepers, foliage gleaners, and antbirds were all about us, feeding on the insects disturbed by the traveling ants. We walked to the edge of a stream, where we saw several more flycatcher species (including that charming pied fuzzball of a bird called the Torrent Flycatcher), wrens, various warblers, and hummingbirds. A short hike up a steep, cleared hillside produced several members of the finch family, as well as doves and a group of Fiery-billed Aracaris. When we returned for lunch, Skutch put out a tray laden with freshly cut local fruits. Immediately it attracted a dazzling display of eight species of tanagers and three honeycreepers.

During our two-day visit with the Skutches I saw over a hundred bird species that were new to me. This was not surprising, as I was exploring an unfamiliar world. Skutch himself, as unusual as his surroundings, was a source of fascination and frustration. Despite his reputation as an ornithologist, he insisted that he was first and foremost a philosopher. Between snatches of information about the unique birdlife of Costa Rica, we were offered innumerable nuggets of his equally unique theology.

Skutch's monographs on Central Amercan birds are classics and not likely to be duplicated.

Motmot in Rain Forest

# Quetzal

Another Costa Rican foray into the wilds immediately followed our visit with the Skutches. We were promised that we could be shown the fabulous Quetzal, sacred bird of the Mayans and Aztecs, that nested in the "backyard" of an acquaintance of Devin's. Shortly after settling ourselves in a San José hotel, we were called on by a Señor Tattenbach, brother-in-law of a Señor Thun (our Quetzal connection.) Evidently he came by to check us out and decide if we were fit for the rugged trip into the mountains. He must have been satisfied, for on the appointed day and hour we were met by a jeep and driven up the mountains for 20 kilometers to an elevation of about 7,000 feet. We arrived at a chaletlike establishment, and were greeted by the Conde and Condesa (count and countess) Tattenbach. Count Tattenbach, the elderly father-in-law of the mysterious Thun, had once been in the diplomatic corps and had fled Hitler's Germany to settle as far from Europe as possible. We found him a gracious host.

After lunch the jeep took us up another 1,000 feet to a corral in the high forest country. Here two horses and a boy name Javier (pronounced hav-ye) awaited us. It had started to rain, and we faced the ride into the wilderness with more than curiosity. We had brought only binoculars, a change of clothing rolled up in a saddlebag, a bottle of Old Grand-Dad, and a borrowed raincoat apiece. Javier, on foot, led the horses and carried a small brass lamp, which held a single candle.

We headed up a steep cow path through a towering cloud forest, beautiful but alien to man. Rain fell in torrents, occasionally interspersed with bright spells. Giant ghostly trees, whose branches were heavily burdened with bromiliads and orchid plants, appeared along the trail, only to vanish when engulfed by waves of vapor. Valleys and hillsides were thick with tangles of bamboo, fifty-foot tree ferns, and giant arums with glistening wet leaves. Several times the trail was so steep and slippery we found it safer to dismount and let the horses feel out the path, unburdened. Neither of us had the remotest idea where we were headed. Looking down the ridge-back slopes through breaks in the mist, we could see steep drops of a thousand feet or more. I crossed my fingers and hoped the horses wouldn't stumble. Luckily they were as surefooted as Javier was inexhaustible. As we passed the Continental Divide at about 9,000 feet in the gathering dusk, the lamp was lit. Beautiful, unfamiliar moths were attracted to the light, beating against it from time to time. I remember silent valleys twinkling with unnumbered fireflies that flashed on and off, almost in unison. We went on and on through the night.

We had left the corral at 3:00 P.M.; by 9:00 I thought we were lost, and was becoming quite concerned. Then out of the black a light appeared and we heard a shout. We had arrived "chez Thun," wet, hungry, and cold. Roderick and Manuela Thun proved to be most friendly and sympathetic to our needs. Their minute chalet provided us with a warm shower and a good dinner. We were then led down a short hill and shown our quarters — a bare room in the dairy, primitive in every respect, but dry and warm. Bedding consisted of thin mattresses laid over straw. There was a colorful primitive altar in one corner, and slimy black leeches crawled up the damp walls.

Conversation revealed that Thun had been an engineer in a Messerschmidt aircraft factory. At the end of the war he came to Costa Rica and married Count Tattenbach's daughter. In this remote spot

... a charming fuzzball ... the Torrent Flycatcher

they kept a herd of Ayrshire milk cows, made a good white cheese, which once a week was transported by horse-drawn wagon down to the city. The Señora was deeply interested in the native Indians and taught them; she had become a dedicated social worker.

The next morning a brilliant sun broke through the mist, and we found ourselves walking about a spectacular Garden of Eden. The great forested cone of Mt. Irazú (11,260 feet) dominated the scene. Rushing streams were bordered by knee-high watercress. Blooming Calla Lilies spread like snowdrifts in the meadows. From the valley came the loud ventriloquial metallic calls of Three-wattled Bellbirds. Scanning the trees with my glasses, I picked up a number of nervous, tail-fanning Collared and Slate-throated Redstarts, a Squirrel Cuckoo, Prong-billed Barbets, and three species of caroling robins.

We were instructed to follow a native boy who knew the local birds and their calls, so I scrambled after him up a steep hillside. Reaching the summit, my eye followed the boy's pointing finger. There I saw, perched motionless on a mossy branch, my first Quetzal. Green-gold with a red belly patch, this female could easily have been mistaken for a bromiliad. I watched the bird in awe for several minutes, then inched my way back down the hill. I could not help recalling the summer before when I had seen the great feathered crown of Montezuma in the Vienna Art Museum. This treasure is composed of 400 long, shimmering green Quetzal plumes, radiating from a brilliant base of tanager and cotinga feathers. It has weathered 400 years of history and, though now rather moth-eaten, it still retains an aura of majesty.

Later, as we were eating our picnic lunch of cream cheese and watercress on homemade bread, a male Quetzal appeared suddenly from a woodpecker hole near the stump of a close-by dead oak. A female soon joined him, and for the next hour we watched, in full sunlight, the courtship of these spectacular creatures, considered by many to be the most beautiful birds in the world. The male cooed and snapped his incredibly long and gracefully curved tail coverts. Leaving the branch in a bounding flight, he soared several hundred feet in the air, banked, and glided back to his perch. Both then alternated entering the nest cavity and removing unwanted debris. When the male entered the hole, several inches of green tail plumes still protruded, gently swaying in the breeze.

*Quetzal in flight...*

My camera and lenses had been left at the Tattenbachs, as I lacked a waterproof carrying case, and today I still curse myself for my neglect. It was the dream of a lifetime for any wildlife photographer.

Later that afternoon we saw another mated pair of Quetzals, but they were less preoccupied with the mating ritual and consequently much shyer.

We spent another night with the Thuns and then departed, following the cheese wagon down the mountains.

I have often wondered how the subsequent eruption of Mt. Irazu in 1963, which brought such devastation to that part of Costa Rica, affected the Thuns and the Tattenbachs. Despite thank-you letters and cards sent at Christmas, neither of us ever heard from them again.

Ocellated Turkey... amongst the stelae...

# Tikal

Mid-August, 1976, found me in northern Guatemala with a small group of earnest birders. Our young leader was Christopher Leahy, working under the auspices of the very active Massachusetts Audubon Society. Five of our ten days' tour were spent at Tikal and its 100 square miles of forest reserve. Leahy was certainly one of the sharpest birders I have ever met. His experienced eyes and keen hearing could pick up a motionless Trogan, a skulking wren in the darkest recesses of the forest, or quickly identify the shrill squeak of a hummingbird. Although I am not a serious bird lister, I did, with his help, add 52 new species on this particular trip.

Oddly enough, my deepest impressions of Tikal came during the late afternoon when walking about alone. Leaving the rather primitive Jungle Lodge cabins, I ambled up a dirt road to the Great Plaza, the heart of a complex of Mayan temples. Highly nervous Agoutis, oddly designed tropical American rodents the size of jack rabbits, with blunt hammer heads and pencil-thin legs, skipped about in the forest openings. A lone, delicate Gray Fox, in immaculate pelage, began his evening hunt, nose to the ground, surprisingly undisturbed by my presence.

I recall passing a strange, elongated shape suspended from the tip of a tree branch, the nest of a Royal Flycatcher, a drab bird with a concealed scarlet crest. Resembling a clump of dried leaves caught in a spider's web, there was no suggestion that the nest was active until the female bird appeared, her bill packed with insects, and vanished into its center. A Slaty-tailed Trogan, lost in shadow, gave his last calls of the day.

I entered the sacred grounds of the Great Plaza at Tikal with its mowed lawns and tall awesome temples. This, the greatest of all Mayan cities, flourished from A.D. 600 to 900, when their civilization mysteriously disappeared and the jungle took over. The last fume-belching bus had swallowed up its tourists and noisily left the scene. All was wonderfully quiet. I had remained with the hope of photographing the late shafts of sunlight climbing the temple steps and bathing the highest carved temple combs in gold. An Orange-breasted Falcon returned to his favorite perch, a dead branch near the temple at Acropolis No. 2. He, too, seemed to be waiting for quiet to return. With the evening flights overhead of parrots and pigeons, perhaps he had hopes of picking up a meal.

A low shaft of sun slipped through a gap in the western forest wall and touched the open lawn. Unexpectedly, three Ocellated Turkey cocks moved from the dimness of the bush into the light, and picked their way among the great engraved stelae stones that were scattered about. Unlike their heavier northern relatives, this species has a changeable bronze sheen that is more green than red. Their forget-me-not blue heads are covered with red warty protuberances, and their longish gray tails are decorated with brilliant metallic eyespots. After scratching the ground and pecking at invisible objects, the trio moved back into the shadows. I was grateful for this fleeting encounter with the only other species of turkey, lasting no more than seconds, yet long enough to marvel at a beauty as fugitive as the sunset. My feeling of awe continued during the mile-long walk down a steep incline and through the dark forest to the main gate. It even survived the explosion of a scolding in Spanish from the cranky guard, who informed me that I had outstayed my welcome and that the area was closed for the night.

The combination of Mayan ruins, only a fraction of which have been uncovered and described, and the spectacular birdlife make Tikal one of the showplaces of the Western Hemisphere.

## Condors

In July, 1978, I joined Peter Manigault, a Charleston friend, on a trip to see the Andean Condor in the wild. We caught a daylight flight from Miami to Lima, Peru. Peter was a fine companion, familiar with the country, at ease with the Spanish language and already acquainted with condors.

In a rented Volkswagen we left the elegant Gran Hotel Bolivar in the heart of Lima, drove through a shocking suburban sprawl of adobe and tin shacks, and took the Pan-American Highway south for 200 miles to the Paracas Peninsula.

Except for scattered glimpses of great ocean combers attacking the coastal cliffs, we saw only a dusty monotone of grays and tans as we traveled the hills and plains west of the Andean spine. It was late in the month, and we were in the middle of the dry winter season. At best, less than a few inches of rain fall annually on this great coastal desert. Occasionally a river, spawned in the mountains, flows westward, irrigating fields along a narrow belt back from the sea, making it possible to raise fine quality cotton.

We approached the Paracas Peninsula at sunset and drove into the grounds of the recently acquired waterfront villa (and future research center) of our host and hostess, Felipe and Maria-Teresa Benavides.

A former diplomat, the aristocratic Señor Benavides maintains that his family has lived in Peru longer than the Incas. An ardent naturalist, he recently won the J. Paul Getty yearly conservation award ($50,000, which he turned over to the Paracas Park) for his efforts to save the endangered vicuña. A large handsome man, in his early sixties, with fiercely penetrating eyes, he exerted an aggressive, overpowering personality. As an ardent conservationist he learned long ago that the way to catch the attention of indifferent politicians was to nag incessantly, speak loudly, and pound the table emphatically. South America as a whole is just awakening to the urgent need for conservation.

Señor Benavides had already developed a vicuña reserve, as well as a million-acre forest park, Manu, on the eastern slope of the Andes. Due to his determined efforts the Peruvian Government has recently established South America's first marine reserve at the Paracas Peninsula, setting aside 120,000 acres of coastal desert and an even larger area of adjacent ocean. The purpose is to save a number of endangered species of seals, a sea otter, the rare Leatherback Turtle and seven species of birds. Unfortunately, there is a lack of adequate funds and world interest in conservation efforts like this.

Included in this coastal reserve are important guano islands. The Incas understood the importance of guano and gathered it for agriculture, valuing it to the extent that they imposed the death penalty on anyone who disturbed the nesting birds. Guano is deposited by cormorants and to a lesser extent by boobies and pelicans. With virtually no rain to wash it away, the accumulations have built up to a depth as great as 180 feet in some places on the islands.

Between 1850 and 1875, 20 million tons of guano were removed from the Chincha Islands (now part of the reserve). Careless handling of nesting birds and overfishing of anchovies (the chief food of the cormorants) have brought the present tonnage to a fraction of

*Condor approaching...*

what it has been in the past. The anchovies, now netted, are converted into fish meal and sold overseas as cattle and poultry feed. Formerly they were used to feed Peruvians, many of whom suffer serious protein deficiencies.

Added to these problems of ignorance and mismanagement is a natural phenomenon that occurs periodically, called "El Niño." During this time (generally midwinter) warm waters from the north push the cold coastal waters far out to sea, taking with them the rich fish life.

Nesting seabirds, unable to range very far, are thus left foodless. The two bad years of 1965 and 1972 caused the guano bird population to drop from an estimated 30 million to less than 3 million. Driving about the Paracas Peninsula we could see hundreds of idle fishing boats nestled together in secluded harbors, their masts resembling a forest of dead trees.

Felipe Benavides took us in his Landrover into the interior of the Paracas Peninsula with its pink sand hills and purple shadows. He drove us along the coast to lookout points where the great condors might be expected to appear.

As the morning fog burned away, the warm sun created thermal updrafts, on which condors (the world's largest flying birds) glide effortlessly over the coast. When pickings are lean in their high Andean retreats, they will fly hundreds of miles to scavenge the coast. Here they search for carrion — dead seal, fish, turtle, or a stranded porpoise.

Seen in the aviary of a zoo, the Andean Condor is a formidable creature — 30 pounds of vulture with a 12-foot wingspan. It often sits hunched on a perch showing white patches of feathers, secondaries and greater wing coverts on the back of huge, drooping wings, a white neck ruff, and a naked purplish head, with a comb on the males. Once rather common all along the Andean range from western Venezuela to Cape Horn, the birds have suffered constant persecution, which has today brought them, like the California species, numbering less than 50 individuals, to the status of endangered species. In some remote mountain villages they are still used for pagan rituals — tied to the backs of bulls or even crucified while still alive.

Señor Benavides stopped the car on the promontory of a high cliff. As I looked over the edge (a drop of several hundred feet) I saw maelstrom seas heaving and crashing. Sea lions clustered in small coves or gathered on sea-washed rocks. Flock after flock of Peruvian Boobies passed by in wedge formations. Beautiful gray Inca Terns with long white mustachios wheeled about ledges, and nesting Red-footed Cormorants crowned rocky islets. Turkey buzzards glided by on upturned tilted wings. Far in the distance, two giant birds, dwarfing the buzzards, approached on horizontal wings. Within seconds they were close enough for us to see their white neck ruffs and the diagnostic, separated primary feathers, expanded like reaching fingers. Now directly above us, the condors suddenly turned their heads, as something caught their attention, and both wheeled in a wide circle over the sea. White back patches stood out sharply, and one could admire the noblest asset of these birds, their supreme accomplishment — flight.

The grandeur and vastness of the surroundings, where the desert meets the sea, were an eloquent setting for these avian giants. Back from circling the sea and over the cliff again, they cast dark shadows, which swept past us following the contours of the pink sands; then they vanished.

We saw perhaps a dozen condors that first morning. Our host, familiar with condors all his life, was still moved by their majesty, their effortless flight. And, like a proud father, he was obviously delighted to have a part in fostering their continued existence.

Inca Terns

SOUTH AMERICA
PUNTA ARENAS
USHUAIA
CARCASS
WEST POINT
NEW
FALKLAND ISLANDS
PORT STANLEY
CAPE HORN
ANTARCTIC CONVERGENCE
DRAKE PASSAGE
SHAG ROCKS
ELEPHANT
CLARENCE
ILES.
S. GEORGIA ISLAND
S. ORKNEY ISLANDS
PALMER PENINSULA
ANTARCTICA

# The Falklands, South Georgia, and Antarctica

WHILE I WAS CHECKING my baggage at Kennedy Airport in November, 1974, for an evening flight to Buenos Aires, a friendly female voice behind me said, "Not you again, John Henry!" Turning around I recognized Barbara Peterson, surrounded by mountains of luggage, camera cases, and clutching a briefcase filled with tickets, passports, and papers pursuant to the routine, thankless role of secretary, courier, and workhorse for her husband, Roger Tory Peterson.

Only four months earlier, when we were cruising the western coast of Greenland, Roger mentioned that a special Falkland Islands, South Georgia, Antarctic trip was forthcoming in December. This turned out to be the trip of a lifetime, in the company of top naturalists as well as talented artists. In a part of the world notorious for bad weather we had the finest weather imaginable. Seas were moderately calm, and ice fields seemed to part before us. At an abandoned whaling station in South Georgia, I talked to a British sailor. He looked at the blue skies overhead and the bay encircled by a wall of scintillating alpine mountains, and remarked, "I've been here for four months, and have not seen a mountain until today."

On an all-day birding trip before sailing we left the giant city of Buenos Aires by bus and headed 150 miles to the town of Monte and its lake. We arrived at our destination about midmorning and parked beside the large lake that borders the town. At Monte I expected at least a hill, but the area was flat as a pancake. The lake is a favorite attraction for naturalists interested in waterfowl. Three species of coots, a jacana, and two gallinules chased each other and grunted in the bordering reed beds, while three species of grebes swam around with great dignity. I had not expected to see Florida specialties like the Roseate Spoonbill, Glossy Ibis, and Limpkin, but they were there. The biggest spectacle at Monte was a congregation of Black-necked Swans. Peterson estimated that there were 2,500 of them. Having been sniped at often from the shore, they kept to the center of the lake out of range of gunshot.

A young Argentine artist, Jorge Rodriquez Marta, joined us at a barbecue lunch by the lakeshore. He had brought along his original drawings for a forthcoming guide to the birds of South America and was anxious to have Roger Peterson see them. Roger, always generous with young, upcoming artists, spent much time over the drawings and was most encouraging. Among his many virtues he has an excellent critical eye and manages always to look for the good points in a fellow artist's work.

At the popular beach resort and harbor of Mar del Plata the Lindblad *Explorer* awaited its passengers. In the ship's lounge there was a friendly exchange of greetings, introductions, and the usual minor crises about misplaced luggage.

I recognized Capt. Hasse Nilsson and was delighted that this fine Norseman would again lead us into dangerous waters. I was also very pleased that the Sewall Pettingills were along, having recently contributed numerous sketches for Sewall's new book *Bird Watcher's America*.

I had long been an admirer of Keith Shackleton and his art, and it was a special pleasure to meet him at last. He is a distant relative of the famous explorer, Sir Ernest Shackleton. Only four years my junior, Keith is boyish, short, athletic, and blue-eyed, with tousled blond hair.

Keith and Sir Peter Scott pursue the same subjects, mainly paintings dealing with waterfowl, clouds, waves, and sails — all in search of "the eye of the wind." It is difficult to compare two talented men, but I believe Shackleton's brush has tackled a wider range of subjects.

For two and a half days rough seas and foul weather confined me to

*Black-necked Swans.*

my cabin. On the morning of December 5, finally feeling myself again, I ventured out on deck. We had reached the Falkland Islands. Bright sunshine broke through the cloud cover as the high headlands of West Point Island appeared ahead. It was not unlike an early spring morning off the New England coast, with the odors of grass, flowers, and earth subtly blending with fresh sea air.

Black-browed Albatrosses, Giant Petrels, and Prions flew about the ship in great numbers. King and Rock Shag Cormorants flew overhead in long lines from shore to feeding grounds. In schools, penguins of possibly five species swam near the boat, but from above their high speed and general similarity made them difficult to identify. Looking down from the height of the deck, I saw them using their flippers as they flew through the clear blue waters below — as any airborne bird might do.

The Falkland Islands lie some 350 miles east of the Strait of Magellan and 800 miles north of the Antarctic Peninsula. The islands divide into two main groups, with at least 250 small islands and islets scattered about. The entire land area is comparable in size to the State of Connecticut. Although claimed by Argentina, they are a British Crown Colony, the southernmost in the world. When talking to an Argentinian, it is wise to refer to them as the Malvinas. For years the two countries have been contesting their ownership. Argentina is now trying the gentle approach of wooing the youth from the islands to the more exciting, sophisticated life of the mainland. In the long run this may turn the tide in Argentina's favor. Certainly neither country wishes to resort to conflict.

The population of the Falklands is about 2,500, with half the people living in its only town, Port Stanley. Though of mixed origin, the people are mainly of Scots-English stock. Sheep raising is the sole industry. Because of the rugged climate, wool here is thick and of very fine quality.

The islands themselves are windswept, treeless, grass-covered, and justly famous for their unpredictable weather. Gale winds blow one day out of five. The birdlife is fascinating for variety of species, tameness, and sheer numbers.

We made our first landing at West Point, a smallish island in the northwest corner of the Falklands. It is privately owned by the Napiers, a conservation-minded family of sheep ranchers. The homestead and shearing sheds huddle neatly together, forming a compound of small buildings in an oasis of Monterey Cypress trees and gorse bushes (then in full flower). The cypresses, planted as windbreaks, were imported from California. They seem to be the only tree capable of withstanding the constant winds in this uncompromising land. Gorse, imported from Britain, formed hedgerows and vast hillside drifts. Its butter-yellow blossoms permeated the air with sweet honey-coconut perfume.

We followed sheep trails over cropped green hills of various grasses and heather locally called "diddle-dee." I stopped many times to photograph remarkably tame Ruddy-headed and Upland Geese. The brown Austral Thrush, a dun-colored version of our American robin, sang a caroling song from atop a gorse thicket.

Flitting about the same bushes were Siskins and Black-throated Finches. Higher in the hills were solitary Rufous-chested Dotterels and Red-breasted Troupials (actually dark meadowlarks with red chests). Long-legged Ground Tyrants, a sooty-colored South American flycatcher, flew from rock to rock ahead of us.

The upward trail ended at a sheep fence, and suddenly the air was full of the raucous calls of penguins. A great amphitheatre sloped down to low sea cliffs, and every available space was occupied by teeming thousands of nesting Rockhopper Penguins. These squat, twenty-inch-high birds argued and fought with flipper and bill over territory, a stolen lump of mud, or a clump of grass.

Black-browed albatross
... lovely creatures to watch

Rockhoppers, like all their relatives, are strictly sea-living birds, which come ashore to breed. They are ruby-eyed, tuxedoed, arrogant, but charming creatures with yellow, disheveled, tufted plumes on the sides of their heads.

Following their deeply cut earth trails among the tussock grass clumps, we walked down to the sea cliffs. When I stopped in their paths I felt like Gulliver, as penguins walked over my boots. Going about their business they would look up at me as if I were some strange, upright sea lion. The rock shelves and large boulders were deeply scored by the claws of unnumbered generations of these birds.

Close to the edge of the cliffs, goose-sized Black-browed Albatrosses, silent and dignified, sat on high, hard mud nests, scorning their noisy neighbors. Settled thus, they are completely tame and can even be touched. Gentle and soft-feathered, they are lovely creatures to watch. Often the mated pairs would bill and coo, sometimes affectionately nibbling each other's necks.

King Cormorants, less regal than the albatross, are nevertheless striking with their blue-black back, forward curled crests, yellow face wattles, and silky white breasts. They were nesting on high ground in the thick of the massed penguins.

Two Wilson's Snipe held their ground in a tussock bog, where I could photograph them easily. Johnny Rock (a nickname for the local and rather rare Austral Caracara) scavenged about looking for eggs or other prey. Turkey Vultures tilted back and forth in the air high above the rocky crags, or roosted on boulders in the strange, dry rock riverbeds that seem unique to the Falklands. Upland geese and sheep were everywhere. I have been told that there are some half million sheep and 10,000 head of cattle on the islands. The geese compete with the animals for grass and are therefore unpopular with the ranchers. Although heavily shot, geese populations remain high.

Before the arrival of man the islands teemed with even more wildlife. However, a century ago whalers did not stop at their commercial exploitation of whales. Fur seals and elephant seals were brought to the verge of extinction. Over three million penguins were boiled down for oil. A story goes that not too many years ago the last colony of the large handsome King Penguin, once numerous, was reduced to a barrel of oil used to waterproof a shepherd's roof.

Recently, a welcome new interest in conservation in the Falklands has proved helpful. Elephant Seals now produce perhaps 5,000 pups a year, and the fur seals have returned. Even a small colony of King Penguins (about thirty-five in 1974) is building in numbers.

Walking the beaches near a sheltered cove, I found Magellanic Penguins very abundant, though shyer and more solitary than other penguins, nesting deep within burrows. Unemployed groups of them huddled together and walked the sheep-cropped lawns, like spectators at a golf tournament.

Two species of crimson-billed oystercatchers, the Black and Magellanic, sought mussels in the tidal pools and coastal rocks. These seemed quite tame.

Heavy-set, blue-gray Flightless Steamer Ducks cruised along the shoreline, gently undulating along with the beds of kelp, trailing behind them flotillas of downy ducklings. Night Herons stalked fish or prawn in rock pools. Most appealing of all were the lovely Kelp Geese. In pairs, they walked the shore, many with newly hatched broods of cotton-white young trailing behind them, tumbling over rocks and scrambling through jungles of kelp stems.

The *Explorer* moved on to two more fascinating islands, Carcass and New Island. The good weather held. I tallied up my list of native Falkland birds and found I had carefully photographed over half of the sixty-one known nesting species.

... Magellanic Penguins ... like spectators

There was much to see and photograph on Carcass Island. I hiked to the edge of a large colony of Gentoo Penguins. Observing them was like watching a soap opera. The villains were the brown, gull-like Skuas who patrolled the border of the colony, hoping to grab a newly hatched chick or an unguarded egg. From each nest colored guano squirts and blotches radiated, reminding me of paintings by Jackson Pollock. Groups of Gentoos, dusty and nest-stained, walked to the sea to swim and to feed, while others, wet and silky clean, burst out of the oncoming breakers like popcorn and waddled back to the colony.

I walked the rocky highland moors, where brown, sparrowlike Correndera Pipits jumped into flight at my feet. From this high vantage point I picked out a pair of Red-backed Hawks (common on the mainland pampas) and a single Cassin's Peregrine Falcon. I crept slowly toward a few Black-necked Swans swimming in a small pond. They took off, but, once airborne, their flight against strong headwinds afforded good photography.

Kelp Geese and young . . .

*... leaving Pembroke Light to starboard ...*

Our last day in the Falklands was spent in Port Stanley. Here we had typical Falkland weather — gale winds and rain squalls with brief periods of sunshine.

A walk along the main street by the harbor thrust one back into a corner of Victorian England — small, neatly painted two-story houses, smoking chimney pots, white picket fences and manicured, colorful gardens. Most front doors opened into a small greenhouse vestibule, crowded with flowering potted plants.

I walked past the red brick Anglican Church, where, near the door on the grass, the upright jawbones of whales made a double Gothic arch. A robed clergyman stood at the doorway shaking hands with his departing congregation.

Farther along a small parade of smartly uniformed military, together with police and scouts, headed toward a granite monument bearing the bronze model of an Elizabethan ship commemorating the battle of the Falkland Islands. It happened to be December 8, the day when, in 1914, a British naval force surprised and destroyed a large German fleet of several capital ships. This was one of the great naval battles of World War I.

Governor General Ernest Lewis, resplendent in full-dress uniform, plumed hat, and rows of medals, escorted his white-gloved wife to the monument for a brief ceremony. Eight thousand miles of ocean separated them from England, but for a brief moment the once great British Empire seemed alive again.

Leaving Pembroke Light to starboard we sailed from the Falkland Islands and headed almost due east to South Georgia Island, making headway through high winds and surging seas. From the stern of the *Explorer* swirls of Prions and Cape Pigeons swung from one side of the ship to the other. Wandering Albatrosses also used the strong winds, for sheer enjoyment it seemed. They were totally at home soaring, banking, diving to within inches of the sea, vanishing behind the ship's wake, reappearing again on motionless wings.

The seas calmed, and light snow began to fall. Two hundred miles west of South Georgia off to starboard appeared what must be the loneliest bit of real estate on earth, the Shag Rocks. These are five black, reaching, twisted fingers, the tallest rising a hundred feet out of the sea. Edging toward them, with the ship's motors almost shut down, we could see the guano-capped peaks crowned with cormorants. Slowly and dramatically great sea swells surged in disturbed eddies at the base of the rocks, for all the world like a drawing by Doré or Dali, terrifying in their bleakness.

With snow still falling and the temperature a cold 20 degrees F., the *Explorer* cruised the northern coast of South Georgia. It was in January, 1775, that England's Captain Cook discovered South Georgia, 110 miles long and about 15 miles wide. Cook described it as "not worthy of discovery, lands doomed by nature to perpetual frigidness, never to feel the warmth of the sun's rays, whose horrible and savage aspect cannot be described."

At first glance the northern coast did have an awesome appearance, but as we entered the fjord that wound its way to the whaling station at Grytviken, the sun appeared. Never before have I seen such magnificence. It was as if the top 6,000 feet of the Swiss Alps rose from the sea. Crystal clear atmosphere accentuated every visible detail.

We tied up to the docks of the abandoned whaling station, whose weathered wooden buildings, rusting machinery, and coiled miles of cable intrigued the eye. Several small, high-stacked, coal-burning whaling ships, now hulk, rested at odd angles along the edge of the water. The factory had been shut down in 1965.

Shag Rocks . . . .

*... South Georgia meadow ...*

Looking over this ghost town from the deck of the *Explorer*, it was not difficult to imagine the factory in operation only ten years before — tall thin chimneys pouring out black smoke, men in spiked boots climbing over bloated whale carcasses, cutting thick strips of blubber and meat to feed the conveyor belts that traveled to the furnaces and grinders. Over this orgy of blood and offal, thousands of seabirds would wheel and feast on waste.

Until recently the whaling industry was so lucrative that investors could double their money in a year. This factory closed down for one simple reason: there were no more whales. Fifty years ago one could see a hundred whales a day in the same area.

A mile from the whaling station was a small British naval outpost. It was here I met a sailor who said that that day he had seen the sun for the first time in four months.

All along the rocky beaches near the factory were whale skulls and bleached piles of bones, solemn relics of the not too distant past. Two- or three-ton Elephant Seals, almost exterminated a few years ago, were now making a comeback. Roger Peterson told us that five years earlier he had seen perhaps ten seals in all. That day we saw several hundred.

On a hillside covered with thick tussock grass, near the abandoned factory, we visited the grave of Sir Ernest Shackleton. Keith Shackleton, in a solemn manner, appropriately placed a wreath on the simple stone marker.

Still attracted to this part of the world, even after his ordeal of 1919, the explorer Shackleton died of a heart attack. His body was taken to Montevideo, but at the request of Lady Shackleton it was returned to South Georgia for burial.

The good weather enabled us to visit several King and Macaroni Penguin colonies, seal rookeries, and many other excellent wildlife areas.

I was most excited to visit nesting sites of the Wandering Albatross in the Bay of Isles. These mammoth birds are as nobly beautiful close at hand as from afar. They sit on their nests as serenely as they fly the wildest and loneliest seas. Small islands are selected for nesting because they provide an open "air field." The ever-present wind makes the area ideal for safe landings and takeoffs.

Few persons have ever walked on these islets, with their thick covering of tussock grass and moss. Foul weather and treacherous seas generally make landing impossible.

With the aid of a rope we scrambled up a high muddy cliff to the open moorland of Bird Island. Dispersed here and there on ridges and hilltops were what appeared, from a distance, to be small snowdrifts. However, my binoculars revealed them to be isolated couples and trios of courting albatrosses. Their nests are built high, like small volcanos of mud and grass. No eggs were yet evident. The incubation period is a staggering 72 days (compared to 21 days for a chicken). Whether courting or sitting aloof on the empty nest, the birds did not resent our close presence. I enjoyed just being close to these great 25-pound seabirds, marveling at their silky white plumage, herringbone marking on wing coverts, great pink bills, and small, gentle eyes.

The courtship ritual is a complex dance that can last an hour or more. First the pair walk about, face each other, nibble at each other's necks, bow, grunt, click their long bills together, make bubbling sounds, walk slowly in circles, and lift their huge webbed feet in slow motion. Finally, both birds stand upright, chest to chest, and extend their long narrow wings in a forward arch, with bills held high in the air. Seemingly exhausted after this lengthy ballet, they may sit and rest before starting the ritual over again. Before pairs are finally mated, several males may court one female.

Often, near the nest, would be a year-old chick, almost as large as its parents. Loose tufts of silky down, blown by the ever-present wind, would still cling among the new smoky-gray feathers. At this age the chick is seldom fed and spends much time exercising its great, gangling, wobbly wings, preparing for the eventual launching. Once a fledgling has mastered the basics of flight, it takes to the lonely sea, where it remains for up to seven years, until mature.

I walked about the undulating moorlands alone. My knee-high rubber boots often became immersed in deep water pockets. Small brown South Georgia Teal in the bog pools were remarkably tame, as were nesting Skuas. Pipits walked the stony beaches searching for insects and, when disturbed, flew away like windblown winter leaves. The South Georgia Pipit is the only songbird found this close to the Antarctic Circle.

Sleeping Elephant Seals...

... courtship dance ... of the Wandering albatross

We visited a great colony of King Penguins on the mainland. They were at the peak of their nesting season. The 80-pound Emperor is the largest of the penguins, but Kings are next in size and more colorful. Their glossy, blue-gray backs and white bellies contrast beautifully with their velvety-black heads and the brilliant orange neck and throat patches. Tens of thousands were crowded together, sitting upright near the borders of well-populated Elephant Seal wallows, which reeked of excreta. The birds gave loud, trumpeting calls that could be heard from a great distance. Their one egg never touches the wet ground; it is tucked into an abdominal pouch that rests on top of the parents' feet. Parents take shifts incubating the egg, a long two-month process. Huddled in groups among adults, or off to one side, were full-sized youngsters about a year old. Covered in brown fluffy down, they resembled castaway teddy bears or small creatures in worn fur coats as they wandered about, like the albatross chicks, abandoned by their parents and seldom fed. They must learn to swim and to feed themselves or perish.

*Light-mantled Sooty Albatross*

At Elsehul harbor we climbed to a Macaroni Penguin colony above a steep grassy bank. As I moved upward on my knees, grabbing clumps of grass, I met a new albatross. Only a couple of feet apart, we faced each other, eyeball to eyeball. Huddled in a small peat cave, it sat on a mossy nest. The smoky-brown head had black eyes half encircled by a white crescent eye-ring. That dark eye with its quizzical eye-ring captivated me. The Light-mantled Sooty Albatross is undoubtedly one of the most beautiful birds in the world. I never knew feathers could have so many subtle, blending shades of gray.

We cruised in a southwesterly direction and were constantly reminded of the proximity of the Antarctic. The *Explorer* bumped ice floes and cut her way through intermittent ice fields. Captain Nilsson announced that he was heading for the South Orkney Islands and he hoped to drop anchor at a small British scientific station on Signy Island.

Exposed to currents generated in the Weddell Sea, the Orkneys are never quite free of pack ice and massive icebergs. However, the good weather and our good luck held. We edged around bergs the size of city blocks and threaded our way around ice-covered islets that showed only bits of exposed rock. At evening we dropped anchor in a protected cove on Signy Island. The sky was heavily overcast. One spotlight on Signy Base illuminated the whole establishment, which consisted of three prefabricated buildings and the usual pile of oil drums. Oil is here the sole fuel for running the generators and other motors and for heating the buildings.

At four in the morning, in bright daylight, we headed ashore in Zodiacs. Never was there a more glorious morning. The air was calm, the temperature at 18° F., and brilliant sunshine lighted up the world about us. In curling scrolls, thin layers of mist flowed along the contours of the mountains.

At the landing we met the handful of bearded men stationed there. Not having seen outsiders for weeks, they were delighted to talk to anyone about anything.

King Penguins ... huddled in groups

Enormous 5,000-pound bull Elephant Seals, magnificent in their ugliness, lay about the small dock area. Some were fighting in the water, others nuzzled close to each other on the rocky beach, and a few giants humped over the ground like grotesque caterpillars. Some managed to lift their bulk onto the tops of piled oil drums to warm in the sun. In various degrees the skins of these seals were peeling in map-shaped blotches. Their thunderous, belching roars reverberated about the glacial amphitheatre of the bay.

I walked the sheltered hillside behind the base. Protected ravines were carpeted with pillows of velvety green moss, and all rocks were blotched with brilliant orange and blue lichen. Flitting overhead, about the ledges and crevasses in the cliffs, were dove-size Snow Petrels, exquisite ghostlike creatures with immaculate white plumage, black eyes like raisins, and stubby black bills. Nesting amongst them were hundreds of handsomely checkered Pintado Petrels. If one approaches their nesting ledges too closely, one finds that they have the unpleasant habit of ejecting a strong-smelling musky oil from their mouths, often with deadly accuracy. Once hit, one has great difficulty washing away the oil and its smell.

Bull Elephant Seals...

*... never quite free of pack ice and iceberg ...*

We then headed for the Antarctic Peninsula and its adjoining islands. The northernmost of these is the South Shetland group — Elephant and its sister island, Clarence, twenty miles away. The 7,500-foot crown of Clarence Island seemed to float in space above the sea mists, resembling a maritime Kilimanjaro.

Elephant Island is that bleak bit of land and ice where in 1916 Sir Ernest Shackleton left his weary crew for a whole year while he, in an open boat, sailed 800 miles to South Georgia for help.

Keith Shackleton commandeered a Zodiac and hunted the coastline for the exact spot where the 22 men had lived. This was not too difficult, as only two small beach coves were fit to occupy. Using the two whaleboats as a roof, the men supported them with walls of rock. Remnants of the piled stone walls are still clearly visible.

On Elephant Island the few corners of rocky coast not exposed to overhead avalanches or occupied by moving glaciers were thickly populated with tens of thousands of Chin-strap Penguins. As is customary with most penguins, they went about their business unconcerned with our presence.

A sleek Leopard Seal moved into the small cove by our landing rock. Here he indulged in a routine but grisly show. Grabbing a swimming Chin-strap in his mouth, he shook it so fiercely that the penguin's skin separated from its body. With another violent twist of his powerful neck, the seal hurled the entire bleeding skin into space like a glove thrown from a hand, and then ate the body.

More good weather followed the *Explorer* as it wound through the spectacular Le Maire Channel. We visited the Chilean, Argentine, British, and Russian scientific stations nearby. Except for overtones of propaganda, the Russians at Bellingshausen Station tried their best to be friendly. They had even anticipated future tourism by opening a small shop that sold fur hats, amber beads, and lacquer boxes. The mess hall walls were covered with prints depicting great moments in the life of Lenin. Here we were served sliced smoked salmon on dark buttered bread with black tea.

We revisited places I had seen eight years before: Almirante Brown, Palmer Station, Hope Bay. None seemed quite the same. The landscape is constantly being rearranged by ice, snowdrifts, and moving bergs.

At the recently renovated American Palmer Station we were told to look for a melanistic Adelie Penguin that had been seen the year before. In a nearby colony the most unlikely lady in our group found it quickly, nesting in the middle of fifty thousand normal black-and-white birds.

We spent Christmas Eve ashore, anchored at Port Lockroy. Several Gentoo Penguins had built their stone nests on stacked piles of whale bones.

About four o'clock two Zodiacs came ashore with cauldrons of steaming Swedish glug (*glögg* — hot mulled wine with aquavit and spices). Passengers and crew gathered together, and the smoking brew was ladled out. Never underestimate the powers of glug out of doors on Christmas Eve in the Antarctic. Ladies of all ages, whose names had not heretofore registered, were now nestled in our arms.

After the initial flush of camaraderie, Captain Nilsson raised his glass and in his good Swedish accent said, ''To all those whom we love, far from here, scattered about the world, we wish them a very Happy Christmas.'' I knew that never again could Christmas Eve find a more dramatic, magnificent, and, yes, spiritual setting, than the ice and snows of Antarctica.

... Gentoo nesting amongst whale bones ...

# Envoi

*I have spent much of my life seeking other Edens – the wilderness, the wonders of nature, the peaceable kingdom.*

*Perhaps I found it in the magnificence of Antarctica or looking into the amber eyes of a lion. Maybe it was hearing the evening chorus of thrushes in northern forests.*

*Perhaps it exists beyond the pollutions of man, or lies only in his dreams.*

*As long as I live I will pursue it – for to me here is where God reaffirms His presence.*